beyond fried rice

Elizabeth Chong

BROLGA
PUBLISHING PTY LTD

Published by Brolga Publishing Pty Ltd
ACN 063 962 443
P.O. Box 959, Ringwood,
Victoria 3134, Australia

Copyright © 1996

All rights reserved. No part of this publication may be reproduced, stored in a retrieval system, or transmitted in any form or by any means electronic, mechanical, photo-copying, recording or otherwise without prior permission of the publishers.

National Library of Australia
Cataloguing-in-Publication entry

ISBN: 0909608423

Printed by Griffin Paperbacks, Adelaide.
Cover Design by Peter Guberek.
Photographs by Brendon Beacom of Lights Photography, Melbourne.
Design and Production by Pro Art Design, Adelaide.

Dedication

I dedicate this book to my Mother - Jenny Lee Wing Young, and to my children - Michael, Katrina, Angie and Richard. My Mother's gift to me was her special kind of Chinese philosophy, patience, and wisdom. Her influence is present in many of the recipes contained in this work.

My gift to my children is in this heritage.

Acknowledgements

My sincere thanks to my publisher, Mark Zocchi of Brolga Publishing, for providing me with the inspiration to re-visit my earliest book, "The First Happiness". Mark's support and enthusiasm encouraged me to take up my pen once more. I was delighted to experience the joys of my first writings again. I am grateful also, to Julie Zocchi, who so expertly edited my many recipes to make the work come together so easily.

I'd like to express my appreciation for the fine contribution made by photographer, Brendon Beacom, of "Lights Photography" in Melbourne, Brendon's artistic interpretation of my cooking was just brilliant.

The "Panda Restaurant", in the Melbourne suburb of Hawthorn, must be given special mention. The proprietor, Simon Mui and his staff have generously given me their assistance and time over many years.

Contents

Introduction	7
The Food Of China	8
To Market To Market	11
The Chinese Kitchen	22
Cooking Methods	25
Rice And Noodles	32
Soups	40
Seafoods	52
Poultry	67
Meats	79
Vegetables	91
Eggs	100
What Is Dim Sum	103
Something Sweet	110
Homestyle Section	117
Regional Cooking Of China	119
Index	141

Introduction

This book is the natural result of my Chinese-Australian heritage. Most of my life has been divided into two parts. I was born in China and my first three years were spent in the small farming village of my ancestors, in the rural outskirts of Canton before my family settled in North Melbourne close to the Victoria Market. My father, with his three brothers, owned one of the largest of the wholesale fruit stores. They were happy times, with a great deal of emphasis on the Chinese extended family system. There was a great deal of comings and goings of aunts, uncles and cousins and lots of family feasts (we found something to celebrate almost every month) and grandmother's birthdays especially, meant exciting days filled with wondrous sights and smells.

My mother's interests centred entirely around my father and her six children and she was frankly puzzled by the complexities of our school lives. As for my brother's preoccupation with Australian Rules football, it was beyond her Chinese comprehension that seemingly intelligent grown men could invest so much time and energy into kicking a small leather ball around a paddock! She failed to see how this was necessary to sustain a productive life. I think this productivity theory governs many Chinese who have spent a good part of their lives in a China largely powered by sheer survival. My mother grew melons between the rhododendrons, and spring onions around the rose buses; frivolity was an extravagance. And so it was that I learnt the value of two different philosophies, two sets of customs and manners, two languages and two cuisines.

In spite of this, or because of it, I cannot be sure, I was always aware of 'being Chinese'. It is something inherited from past generations, tales of old, folk songs of legend and myth, of emperors and dynasties. All these create a strong sense of identity and no matter where the Chinese make their home, they may be scattered to distant places, a sense of unity binds them all together.

A culinary career was probably inevitable for me. My father was the first to manufacture Chinese food on a commercial scale to supply the Chinese food trade, and was responsible for introducing under the Wing Lee label, the dim-sim and the chicken roll to the Australian take-away market. He wore the crown of 'Chicken Roll King' with amusement and delight. Another first, was the bean sprout factory, producing many tons of fresh bean sprouts for the retail market and for Melbourne's many Chinese restaurants.

There was always a steady succession of Chinese cooks coming and going from our house. Energetic discussions of food and the preparation of it, were never ending and it seemed entirely normal that everybody possessed this passionate interest in good food.

The Western world has long been fascinated by the Chinese diet. In Australia, fried rice and dim sims are household words and in America, there is a restaurant that boasts 'genuine San Francisco chop suey'!

My family are my most enthusiastic cooking critics and many of my new recipes are first tested on them before they are included in any of the courses for students.

I had never planned to spend my days (and nights) around a wok! This, however, seems to have been my destiny, as today more than 20,000 students have become woven into the fabric of my life, enriching me with many beautiful friendships and memories.

I sincerely hope my readers will gain much joy and satisfaction from the recipes, both in the preparation and in the eating! Affectionately I salute you, as you start your journey of a thousand miles. Come with me now, as you take your first step.

The Food of China

'The appreciation of good food, like the appreciation of good music, is an unmistakable sign of culture'.

Lin Yutang

Anyone wanting to prepare Chinese food should keep in mind that food to the Chinese is not just something pleasurable, nor is it just to stave off hunger; food to the Chinese is life in every sense of the word. It gives pleasure certainly, but more than that, it is a symbol of all good things, luck, prosperity, virtue and goodwill. Each time a Chinese eats his meal, he is strengthening body, mind and soul; he is possibly preventing future ills and curing present ones. 'Heaven loves the man who eats well.' Confucius in his wisdom, has said that 'food is the first happiness.'

There is an almost religious obsession among Chinese in their concern and pursuit of this happiness. The 8,000 or so restaurants in Hong Kong are central institutions where the local Chinese virtually celebrates his life from the womb to tomb. Parents celebrate the birth of a child with relatives and friends at a restaurant. His graduation from school, birthdays, wedding and even his death will be celebrated at a restaurant. Business is struck, contracts sealed. The way of goodwill is by way of the stomach. It has been observed that the Chinese live to eat the English eat to live.

There is an old form of greeting that asks 'Have you eaten yet?' The inquiry is not an invitation to dinner, but is a way of showing concern over the well-being of the other. Friendship and food are inseparable. 'Happiness is merely a matter of digestion' says Lin Yutang and Confucius is said to have divorced his wife because her cooking did not meet his high standards.

Sheer necessity has resulted in a 'waste not - want not' philosophy that has produced amazing results in the kitchen. Nothing is thrown away, melons are peeled and the peels dried in the sun to make tasty additions to soups and other dishes, the seeds are dried and salted and enjoyed as tidbits, while the melon flesh can be cooked in a variety of ways.

Perhaps it is because the Chinese are ever mindful of the miseries of times of want that they are so concerned with the quality and the presentation of their food. I never cease to admire the Chinese ingenuity that makes so much out of so little, 'to make the best out of what there is' might be a Chinese philosophy of life.

This thriftiness coupled with amazing ingenuity probably has two sources; firstly the constant struggle against adversity - China has long been familiar with uncertainties of crops, of famine and floods and, secondly her history has produced a cuisine so refined that it could only have evolved from many long years of culture and civilisation. China has the oldest culture on the face of the earth. It is little wonder then, that the Chinese have acquired a preoccupation with their food, a philosophy that states 'eating is the only joy that spans the entirety of a man's lifetime.' To this end then, the preparation and the eating of food has been elevated to the high and honourable art it is.

The Chinese believe that life is governed by the balance of the two great opposites - Yin and Yang. These do no oppose but complement each other, if one is to be happy, then there must be the right balance of these elements; any imbalance causes illness of both body and soul. Broadly, Yin is that which is female, negative, dark and cold, for example, the moon, night, water - these are Yin elements. Yang is that which is male, positive, bright and hot. The sun, day and fire are Yang elements. The Chinese herbalist will feel your pulse to determine which element has the upper hand and prescribe through the proper diet of food and herbs just how matters can be corrected. I well remember mother's and grandmother's constant lectures on the evils of too many 'heating' or 'cooling' foods, this seemed to dominate and frustrate my life as a small child cultivating a devotion to potato chips, licorice straps and doughnuts! My school friends seemed to survive quite well, it seemed to me, on great quantities of 'heating' foods every day. However, I bow to ancient knowledge and now to wisdom of old age and add my voice to those gone before.

In the matter of food, Yin foods are basically low-calorie foods, fruits, leafy green vegetables, clear liquids and Yang foods are all meats, particularly red meats, nuts, root vegetables, oils and animal fats. Interesting to note, is that brandy is considered to be heating and whisky and beer to be cooling. It is not that simple, however, as all food possesses some of both elements and the balance can be changed by the way it is cooked. Deep-frying, for example, 'yangatises' any food. Every dutiful Chinese mother knows instinctively if there is an imbalance of Yin or Yang in her family and prepares her family meals accordingly. If your husband is irritable and cranky, try reducing his Yang intake and if the children are tired and listless, increase it.

So food is medicine, and medicine is food. The Chinese pharmacy looks like a food shop and the food shop looks like a pharmacy. This happy confusion makes medicine less of a medicine and food more of a food. Some of our best soups are in fact, taken as medicine, using prescribed herbs and are enjoyed as much for their flavour as for their restorative powers. A popular soup found in a ready-mix pack can be found on the shelf of every Chinese store. Directions are on the packet with very clear advice telling of untold benefits. The advice goes like this: 'This is an excellent tonic soup for keeping good appearance, soothing lungs and stomach, strengthening spleen, anti-rheumatism, promoting kidneys, relieving heart.'

Then there is another one that reads like this: 'This is good for the following complaints: Feebleness due to age and during convalescence, physical disability and after serious illness, and premature senility; lassitude, over-fatigue, and neurasthenia; poor appetite, loss of weight, and falling of hair. Indeed it is an ideal tonic for male and female all the year round.'

I think it would be quicker to list what these soups don't do! Chicken soup is always regarded as restorative, especially as there is always a fair amount of ginger root cooked with it, but I do have my doubts as to the efficacy of duck soup, which is reputed to being sufficiently powerful to reunite estranged husband and wife! Bird's nest soup with snake meat is said to restore male vigour, as does the gall bladder of snake and ginseng root. I think the effect would be accumulative, rather than instantaneous, so a sudden change of diet is not recommended unless you can get regular supplies! Even our teas are drunk, not just for pleasure, but for good health and are said to 'have remarkable effects in arousing spirits, mitigating intoxication, quenching thirst, dispersing heat, helping digestion and cleansing the bowels.'

I know the English have meanings for flower, roses mean love - they probably have more love for flowers than food - but the Chinese (you guessed it) attach meanings to foods instead. Pomegranates, with all their seeds, symbolize fertility; lotus seeds symbolize male fertility. Peaches represent immortality, or long life, tangerines mean good luck, noodles longevity.

Ducks are an emblem of felicity, since they are usually found in pairs, indicating conjugal colouring, usually develop a strong attachment for their mates and will pine and die away if separated. Fish are a symbol of wealth and abundance. Phonetically, the Chinese word 'yui' means superfluity. As fish swim in pairs, they also signify faithfulness and regeneration.

I have eaten Chinese food in many parts of the world, some has been very bad, much has been very good. After all these years, I am still fascinated with my own native cuisine. With each experience, I am still discovering new delights - the art seems inexhaustible. I am sure this is so, because the Chinese cuisine is brilliant in its ability to adapt to any circumstance. Plain food can be made exciting, tough meat can be made tender, much can be made of a little. The Chinese cook will accept what he has and make the most of it. And where the Chinese have settled in countries far distant from their native land, their food has taken on the characteristics of their adopted country - local ingredients are cooked 'in Chinese' and the result is always imaginative, innovative and delicious!

A short while ago, I revisited China, and found some surprises! I have sought out Chinese restaurants in Europe and found good ones in unlikely places like a ski resort town in Austria; I was kept busy covering the many distinctly different eating places in London and was alternately impressed and disappointed with the standard of Chinese cuisine in America. Hong Kong still fascinates me with its exciting menus and many places to visit and Taiwan features excellent food from the different provinces of China. Last, but in no way least, are Australia's Chinese restaurants. Take a bow, my Chinese compatriots, the overall standard of food, service and cleanliness offered in Australia, is more than equal to anywhere I have eaten in the world. I am proud to be associated with the Chinese cuisine in Australia. World peace may yet be achieved, not around the conference table, but around the dining table!

If Yin and Yang are the two great opposites in life, then perhaps East and West are the two great opposites also; opposites that are complementary and not conflicting. They say that opposites attract.

To Market to Market – Chinese Style

If you are at all serious about cooking Chinese food and you are aiming for authentic results, then you should make a trip every so often into the Chinatown of your capital city. We are fortunate too, that some excellent Chinese stores are now in some of our suburbs.

I enjoy shopping in Chinese stores. There is a liveliness there that is lacking in the sterile modern supermarkets. When I am in the East, I have such a fascination for the local food stalls and market places that I am sure I spend more time among the fish, chickens and vegetables than I do anywhere else!

Because of the evergrowing interest in Chinese food, almost every possible ingredient for Chinese dishes is sold in Chinese shops in Australia. Chinese vegetables such as snow peas, Chinese broccoli, spinach, Chinese cabbages and bean sprouts are grown locally in each city and even when some are out of season, they are flown in from another state.

Dried and Preserved Ingredients

These ingredients are used sparingly, but are important if the dish is to have the characteristic flavours intended in the recipes.

Fresh Ingredients

There is a Chinese saying 'if it moves, it can be cooked' and another saying from the Cantonese, that 'if its back points to heaven, you can eat it.' Mercifully we humans are saved from the cooking pot! I heard recently that 'if you give a chicken to a Chinese, he'll eat everything but the feathers and if the Chinese don't eat the feathers, nobody can.' He was not exaggerating! Equally important though, is the quantity and freshness of the ingredient. In this there can be no compromise.

Meats

Pork: The Chinese butcher shop is 99 per cent lean pork and to the Chinese, meat means 'pork.' Meat is not generally eaten for bulk, but rather for adding flavour and interest to a dish. Consequently, when meat is a little fatty, then the Chinese do not mind, as they eat only small portions at a meal and a certain amount of fat adds to the succulence of a dish.

Lamb / Mutton: Lamb is seldom used by the Chinese because of its strong smell. A little is eaten in the north because of the influence of Mongolia and Tibet.

Beef: Beef dishes are gaining popularity due to the influence of the West. Use only the best tender cuts for stir-frying.

Poultry

Chicken: Poultry is next in importance, with chicken more in demand than duck because of its versatility. Like the pig, the chicken lives happily in the farmyard, picking up scraps of food and even offers eggs to the family as an added bonus.

Chicken is well-known in both Western and Chinese cooking for being easily digestible and nutritious and in both cuisines the methods of cooking chicken are numerous. Like the pig, every part (except the feathers) can be eaten. And the Chinese warning 'Do not let it die in vain' is always heeded by the cook.

Duck: Duck is very highly regarded in Chinese cuisine, but methods of cooking are not as diverse as for chicken. Duck possesses a stronger flavoured meat with a distinctive odour and therefore does not combine easily with other foods. My own favourite duck recipes are stewed or steamed duck cooked long and gently in pieces; one of my favourite soups is twice boiled duck with tangerine skin. More famous is the universally acclaimed Peking duck dish of the north.

One of the most charming sights of the Chinese countryside (and the New Territories of Kowloon) are the many duck farms with the baby ducklings dipping and diving among the lotus flowers in the ponds and lakes. Another duck speciality I had almost forgotten to mention is the salted dried duck. These are the curious flattened ducks you see hanging suspended from the books in the Chinese store. Nanking is famous for preserved ducks, which as yet I have not tasted, but I am very partial to our Cantonese version. Chopped into bite-size pieces and steamed over the rice, it is guaranteed to bring tears of joy to any Chinese who has been deprived of this pleasure for any length of time.

The Chinese word for duck is 'arp', which is exactly the sound the duck makes.

Goose: Goose is not often eaten in Australia, but is favoured more in Europe and Asia. In China and Hong Kong, roast goose with its crispy chestnut skin is a popular speciality.

Pigeon, Squab and Quail: These birds are offered as a restaurant speciality rather than an everyday food. Minced, roasted or fried, they make interesting and different dishes to try. Pigeon soup with special Chinese herbs is an expensive broth often chosen as a soup to celebrate an elderly person's birthday, as it is considered to be a tonic and a restorative.

Seafoods

Freshwater fish is most favoured in China - the Chinese carp, stonefish, pomfret, garoupa, sole and bream are greatly enjoyed. Fish has always been important to the Chinese for we learn that the Chinese were making fish nets and using the finer techniques of fishing almost 3000 years BC. China has a long and varied coastline with many swiftly flowing rivers, lakes and central regions in which freshwater fish abound.

My mother told me she was the village fishing champion. As a young girl she would go fishing in nearby canals and streams and with her hand tease the fish. At the exact moment she would scoop it up in the palm of her hand and triumphantly take it home for the family dinner.

It is hard to improve on the fish cooked the Chinese way. The Chinese cook seeks to bring out to the fullest the natural sweetness and moistness of fish and destroys any 'fishiness' with the skilful use of fresh ginger and spring onions.

I remember with amusement one Chinese chef originally from one of the floating restaurants in Hong Kong. We took him to the Victoria Market to show off our Australian fresh fish, but his amazement turned to dismay when he discovered they were dead!

Good fish from our Australian fish markets include: bream (silver and black), snapper, gurnard, flathead, flounder, Murray cod, Murray perch, garfish, gemfish and all shellfish and crustaceans. Barramundi, king fish, harpuka, trumpeter, rock ling, blue eye and pike are also excellent.

Vegetables

The world over recognises the supremacy of the Chinese in the area of cooking vegetables. With the current vogue for health food, the Chinese method of cooking vegetables and particularly green vegetables for only a few short minutes retains freshness, greenness and all the beneficial qualities of the vegetables. Vegetables cooked 'in Chinese' are the answer to a vegetarian's dream.

It is no accident that the Chinese have such a concentration of vegetables in the diet, 80 per cent of China's people are engaged in agriculture, the Chinese farmer maintains a high productivity level by rotating two or three crops a year on the same field. His instinct for economy is allied with unfailing strength and diligence and he seeks in every way to make maximum use of every inch of land he owns. The farmer makes certain that he grows a steady crop of legumes, for these vegetables provide nourishment for his soil as well as for humans. The most important legume is the soya bean, the miracle bean that offers oil, milk, bean curd and sauce.

An enormous diversity of plants are cultivated in China. One of the most vivid memories I have of China recalls the wide green, cool rice paddies stretching for endless miles. Farmers, coolie hats protecting them from the noon sun, guide their faithful and diligent water buffalos through the fields. Vines heavy with melons of every description cover and hang down from every little building in sight. Sweetcorn, beans, cabbages of every description, spinach, celery and broccoli are so incredibly lush and beautiful, I feel they should be immortalised in songs of praise.

Not only has the good earth been given to the Chinese farmer, but duck and fish ponds abound. Swamps and any nearby water areas are used to grow water chestnuts and lotus plants. In the home, he cultivates bean sprouts and in his garden he will probably make good use of the wild bamboo.

Australia enjoys a variety of climates and soil conditions similar to those of China and produces a wonderful supply and variety of vegetables all the year round. Europeans and Americans are openly envious of the continuous supply of our fresh vegetables and fruits and every Australian ought to make the best possible use of these gifts from Mother Nature.

What vegetables can the Australian cook use in Chinese recipes? Any vegetable, if fresh, is good for Chinese cooking - all you need is knowledge, goodwill and a little imagination!

Rice

Rice is the staple food of China and is cultivated throughout the country especially in the southern province of Kwangtung, where the temperature is mild and sub-tropical. Further north, there is a greater consumption of wheat and millet as a grain food.

It may be surprising to learn that there are several hundreds of varieties of rice; each crop varying because of the many regions where it has been cultivated, differences in soil and climatic conditions and seasons.

Less well-known is glutinous or sticky rice, used in the preparation of sweets, puddings and as stuffings.

A favourite rice meal is conjee (or jook) where the rice is cooked until the grains are 'broken down' and a smooth thick gruel is the result.

Rice is also ground down to make flour for steamed pastries, rice noodles and even cosmetic face powder.

China depends on rice as her principal food and the cultivation of rice is her most important crop. There are plans to re-educate the Chinese to eat more wheat, in the form of noodles, dumplings and bread, so that China's rice may be a valuable export commodity. Certainly noodles are much loved and even Western-style bread is gaining popularity (particularly with the young), but I doubt if the Chinese can ever be weaned off rice as the staple.

Whenever I am away for a time when I have not had rice, I have a feeling of vague discontent until someone gives me a bowl of rice and the malady is fixed!

Eggs

Because we have a lot of chickens in China, it follows that we have a lot of eggs. Like any other cuisine we regard them as a valuable source of nutrition and use them in a variety of ways, but always in the company of other foods. That is to say, I am not aware that Chinese eat eggs simply for their own sake, as in most other parts of the Western world.

Eggs are a great standby; when an extra dish is needed in a hurry, an omelette is my first thought. Beaten in soups to make 'egg flowers' they not only add nourishment but enhance the appearance of the soup and are of course invaluable as binders in cakes and puddings. Hen eggs are most often used, followed by duck eggs and to a lesser extent, quail and pigeon eggs.

A word here for the curious about the ancient one-thousand-year-old-eggs. No, they are not that ancient, but they are about 100 days old. They are duck eggs that have been thickly coated with a mixture of lime, salt and ash, and then placed in a dark cool container (the large attractive dragon decorated jars seen in some of our decorating shops) for almost three months. In that time (as long as nobody in the family indulges in mischievous gossip) the eggs will be preserved. The lime works on the eggs and affects the curing. The egg is now a beautiful iridescent blue-green colour not unlike a black opal and the texture and the flavour reminds me a little of a ripe avocado pear. The flavour is surprisingly pleasant, though somewhat rich and one or two bitefuls eaten with slices of raw pickled ginger are enough as a 'starter' in a dinner menu.

Duck eggs are also preserved in a brine solution for about three weeks and make a tasty addition to soups and steamed meat dishes. Yolks may be dried in the sun and are used in special cakes and pastries such as the festive moon cakes in August.

The Pantry

Abalone: Japan leads the field in this area and is Asia's biggest supplier. Australia, Africa, Mexico and USA also export abalone to the East.

This shellfish is so highly prized in Asia that it remains one of the most expensive dishes on every menu. In its dried form it requires many long hours of preparation and because it is considered to be the best quality, it commands astronomical prices. However, fresh, frozen or canned abalone is still very highly regarded by connoisseurs.
To store: Abalone in its dried form keeps indefinitely. Canned abalone: Use immediately once it has been opened.

Agar agar: A Chinese gelatin used as a setting agent and produced from seaweed. It is sold as translucent 'threads' or in flat sheets. Read accompanying directions, but you

might find gelatin easier to handle.
To store: Keeps indefinitely on pantry shelf.

Anise, star anise: Star anise is the shape of an eight pointed star, hence the name, and has a strong anise (licorice) flavour. It is used to flavour some meat and poultry dishes and is also an ingredient of five-spice powder.
To store: It will keep indefinitely in an airtight container in the pantry.

Baby corn: Miniature ears of corn on the cob come from Taiwan and Bangkok. They need no further cooking and make an attractive addition to dishes featuring vegetables.
To store: Same as for bamboo shoots.

Bamboo shoots: The bamboo plant is a great gift to the Chinese people. Not only do we make use of it as a valuable raw material in construction and in a variety of products from furniture to chopsticks, but the first tender young shoots of the plant are cut and gathered for eating purposes. Fresh bamboo shoots are a prized delicacy in the East, but the canned variety are still good. They are succulent, yet delicately crunchy not unlike young celery and their porous quality absorbs the flavours of other ingredients cooked with them. I can never prepare bamboo shoots without thinking of Su Tung Po, one of China's great poets of the 11th century, who was apparently renowned as much for his cooking as he was for his literary genius. Included in a collection of short poems is a recipe for a soup (it is perfectly natural for Chinese intellectuals to have a passion for fine food). Bamboo and pork feature in this soup and so he preceded his instructions with these lines:

> 'Lack of bamboo makes one vulgar,
> Lack of pork makes one thin,
> In order to avoid vulgarity and slenderness,
> Have bamboo and pork now and again.'

To store: Remove the bamboo shoots from the can to a container, cover with cold water and keep in the refrigerator. Change the water every other day and they will keep for several weeks at least.

Bean Curd: This is made from soy beans and is a rich source of protein, so much so that it is often called in China 'poor man's meat'. The soy bean itself is sometimes called 'the cow of China', as it provides so much for man. Western patrons of Chinese restaurants are now familiar with the soft fresh bean curd cakes similar to custard, sometimes added to soups, other times braised or deep-fried as a companion to other ingredients. Not usually known to the Westerner are the other forms of bean curd - dried into sheets or sticks, or fermented into highly flavoured sauces. Dried bean curd is simmered in hot water for 30 minutes then added to meat, vegetable or soup dishes. A wonderful product for vegetarians - soy bean products have been skilfully used to great advantage for centuries.
To store: The fresh variety can be kept in the refrigerator for about one week if covered with cold water. Change water daily.

Bean Paste, Hot: This very hot and slightly salty paste is made from soya beans, chillies and oil. It is used more often in northern cooking.
To store: Keeps indefinitely in jar in refrigerator. No substitute.

Bean Pates, Sweet: These are purees of the red or black beans and are used as fillings for sweet pastries and dumplings. Other sweet fillings are made from lotus root and coconut.

Bean Sprouts (guar choy): These are the white tender shoots of the mung bean.

Keep covered with fresh cold water in the refrigerator and they will keep for several days.

Black Beans: Salted fermented black soya beans, the size of a pea. They have a strong pungent flavour and are generally crushed and used with fish or beef.
To store: They will keep indefinitely in an airtight container.

Broccoli, Chinese (gai larn choy): A great favourite for home and restaurant cooking. Chinese broccoli has slender stalks unlike the Italian type and instead of the green bunches of flowers, it bears small white flowers. Italian broccoli is also used.

Brown Bean Sauce (min si jeung): A pungent, salty sauce important in some meat dishes, usually 'red cooked' (stewing) dishes, where it gives a characteristic colour as well as flavour. Used for roasting ducklings and often as an important marinade for barbecuing pork. It is surprisingly good with potatoes.
To store: Keeps indefinitely in jar. No substitute.

Cabbage, Chinese White (buk choy): There are two varieties of this cabbage. The most common type has a dark green leaf and a white, crisp stalk. The other variety, has slender stalks and small white flowers (choy sum). Both are good for stir-frying.

Cabbage, Tientsin (song buk choy): A pale spring green cabbage, tightly packed like young celery. Delicately sweet in flavour and used in soups and stir-fried dishes. Usually sold by weight in Chinese stores.

Chillies, dried: These are dried whole peppers. They can be very hot, but the seeds can be removed for those preferring a milder dish.
To store: Keep dry in a container.

Cooking Oil: The Chinese prefer peanut oil. It imparts the right flavour for our food and I recommend that you 'cook' your oil first, then re-bottle it. Simply pour the oil from the bottle or tin into your wok and cook over moderately high heat until the oil just begins to smoke. Turn off heat and allow the oil to cool before re-bottling. The oil takes on a nuttier flavour and the cooking increases its keeping qualities. The added benefit is that it heats up very much more quickly in the wok when you are cooking and that it is also instantly ready when you need extra cooked oil at times. You can substitute safflower, nutro or maize oil.

Cornflour: Is used for thickening in Chinese dishes. In the East, lotus root powder and potato flour is sometimes used. Plain flour is too heavy as a thickening agent.
To store: Keeps indefinitely.

Coriander (yuen sai): Chinese parsley, also known as cilentro. This pretty green herb with flat, serrated leaves and fine stalks has a highly aromatic flavour and is used in garnishes and/or as a flavouring agent. Good in fish, poultry and egg dishes. Western parsley is not a good substitute, except as a garnish.

Dates, Red: Wrinkled red pods the size of a small almond which swell plump and round after soaking. Red dates have a distinct musky sweet flavour not unlike that of a prune. They are used in soups, braised chicken dishes and as a sweet filling for buns and pancakes.
To store: These keep in an airtight container indefinitely.

Fagara (also known as Szechuan Pepper): A fragrant pepper, grown in the province of Sichuan. Should be roasted lightly in a dry pan, then crushed.
To store: Keeps indefinitely on pantry shelf.

Fish, salted: The taste and smell of salted fish is familiar to every Chinese home and remains forever as one of the little 'strong' dishes to be enjoyed with plain steamed rice or conjee, especially at breakfast times. It comes salted and dried, salted or canned, or bottled in oil (like sardines). Sometimes salted fish is steamed on top of the rice as the rice is completing its steaming and sometimes it is shallow-fired until the bones are crisp and crunchy. It has a powerful taste and a little goes a long way.

Fish Soy: A thin light brown sauce made from dried, salted fish. Salted and pungent, it is used as a seasoning, particularly in steamed meat dishes.
To store: Keeps indefinitely in bottle.

Five-spice Powder (spice of five fragrances): An aromatic ready-mix of five Oriental spices - cloves, fagara, fennel, star anise and cinnamon. When included in a recipe, only a pinch of this highly fragrant powder is needed. Used in roasting meats and poultry.
To store: Keeps indefinitely on pantry shelf.

Fungus, Cloud Ear: In the same family as the mushroom. Tree fungus, wun yee which translates as 'cloud ears' and after 30 minutes soaking in warm water resembles perfectly shaped ears. They are fairly bland in flavour and are enjoyed more for their texture than anything else as they are slightly crunchy yet gelatinous, a rare combination you will agree! They add visual interest with their unusual shape and colour.
To store: They will keep indefinitely in an airtight container.

Garlic: Almost as important as ginger, fresh garlic is used for many dishes, especially for beef. Use only fresh garlic, as old garlic imparts a nasty odour and taste to food.
To store: Same as for ginger.

Ginger (fresh root): Indispensable for the Chinese cook. Ginger freshens meat, especially seafoods and poultry and imparts and indefinable sharp sweetness to the cooking oil and to soups.
Older ginger root has thick, rough skin and possesses a strong flavour suitable for soups and slow cooked meat dishes. Tough skin may be carefully removed, but do not cut too deeply, as much of the flavour lies directly under the skin.
To store: Same place as garlic, onions, potatoes.

Ginger, Sweet Mixed: These are selected vegetables and melons used in sweet and sour dishes and the juice can be used with or instead of vinegar in certain dishes. They are available either in cans or jars, and if covered with the juice keep for many months in the refrigerator.

Golden Needles (lily flowers): The gold-coloured buds of the tiger lily with a sweet musky flavour. They are used in dishes with fish, poultry or vegetables. They are often used in conjunction with tree fungus and dried bean curd, to create a typical vegetarian dish.
To store: Golden needles keep indefinitely in an airtight container.

Herb Mixture (look mee or ching po liang): A ready-mixed packet of six selected herbs to make a distinctive soup. Chinese barley and lotus seeds feature to make a 'cooling' or 'yin' soup. The herbs are gently simmered for about 2 hours with chicken or pork to make a very tasty and nourishing soup.
To store: Keeps indefinitely in jar.

Hoi Sin Sauce: Another famous Chinese sauce which has a 'savoury sweetness' and is often used in pork, chicken an shellfish dishes. It is the delicious sauce served with Peking duck.
To store: Keeps indefinitely in jar.

Lotus Root: Lotus root is the tuberous root of the lotus plant or water lily plant and looks a little like sweet potato. It is versatile being used in soups, stir-fried dishes, here it combines well with meat or vegetables, and is sometimes combined with honey or sugar and enjoyed as a sweet dish. It has an attractive appearance because when the stem is cut, the hollow passages running lengthwise form a pretty lacy pattern of holes in each slice. Lotus was cultivated in the lakes and moats of the palaces of the Forbidden City in Peking, where the flowers enhanced the beauty of the surroundings. On a spiritual level, the plant is held as sacred, as the white flower springs from the muddy waters, pure and undefiled, representing the external struggle of man to attain enlightenment and perfection in the midst of darkness. For the more pragmatic, the lotus plant is significant, because every part of the plant, root, seeds, stem fruit and leaves is an important source of food or medicine.

To store: Same as for bamboo shoots.

Lychees/Longans (cousin to the lychee): A reddish-brown skinned fruit, when peeled, reveals an ivory fruit. The fresh variety is like a luscious, sweet grape with the fragrance of a freshly picked rose. Fresh lychees are in limited supply in Australia but widely available in cans.

Mandarin Peel, Dried: More specifically called tangerine peel in China. They are pieces of sun-dried mandarin peel and are quite expensive to buy. They give a unique flavour to certain dishes especially stewing and duck dishes.

Marrow, Chinese (dit gwar): A green skinned melon with a 'fuzzy' skin. The flesh is sweeter and crunchier than English melon and is good in clear soups.

Melon, Bitter (foor gwar): A jade green melon about the size of a small cucumber, with a pebbled skin. The skin is not peeled, but the pith and seeds are removed before stir-frying. It has a decidedly bitter flavour which teams well with meats and black beans. It is also available in cans.

Melon, Tea (char gwar): A sweet amber-coloured pickle which when shredded or minced is added to steamed meats or congee (jook).

To store: In a glass container indefinitely in the refrigerator.

Melon, Winter (doong gwar): A large, round green-skinned melon with a pale green-shite flesh. It resembles a watermelon. The melon has a delicate tasting flesh. It is often featured in restaurants as a gourmet soup, particularly when the flesh is scooped out and combined with other ingredients and served in the whole melon.

Mushrooms: Dried mushrooms or black mushrooms are beloved by the Chinese and used in a great variety of ways. They are graded for size and thickness and although they are quite expensive, the Chinese home always has a supply. They are soaked for approximately 45 minutes in warm water in which time they will become spongy and bouncy and return to their original size. Then they can be used, sliced or whole, as a valuable ingredient in many dishes.

To store: In their dried form they will last indefinitely in an airtight container.

Mushrooms, Straw: These are a little like French champignons, although I do think they are much more interesting. They have a delicate taste and an intriguing shape. They are used as a 'contrast' ingredient in a dish providing added interest. They are also available dried, but the canned variety loses very little from the fresh ones.

To store: For the canned variety, store the same as for bamboo shoots. For the dried variety, store in an airtight container and keep in the pantry.

Mustard Greens (gai choy): A jade green vegetable with a slightly bitter flavour and used in beautiful clear soups like bean curd soup. It can be stir-fried and is sometimes known as leaf mustard.

Noodles: A great variety of dried noodles are available. Most noodles are made from wheat flour and eggs (yellow). Many of the white-coloured noodles are made from rice flour and there is the vermicelli (cellophane) noodles produced from the mung bean flour. Like pasta noodles they come thin, wide or in flat ribbons. They must be boiled for a few minutes according to the recipe before being used in soup or as stir-fried noodle dishes. Fresh noodles are more readily available now in many Chinese stores.

Oyster Sauce: This rich, velvety sauce is made from dehydrated oysters and soy sauce. It is used in gourmet cooking and goes well with chicken, beef and egg dishes. Although made from oyster, the smooth velvety sauce does not possess a 'fishy' taste and is popular with almost everyone. Like all good things, use with discretion.
To store: Keeps indefinitely in the bottle, but is best if refrigerated.

Plum Sauce: Made from Chinese sour plums and seasoning ingredients. It is a thick golden sauce and is used as a condiment in a similar way to chutney. It is a good mixer with other sauces such as hoi sin sauce and makes an interesting flavouring agent or dip. Used sometimes for Peking duck. Sold in cans or jars.
To store: Keeps indefinitely in jar.

Prawns and Shrimps: These should also be fresh or fresh frozen (never boiled first). Look for flesh that is firm and slightly blue-grey in colour. You will need to remove the black gritty thread along the back before cooking. Frozen fresh prawns from China usually have this already removed.

Preserved Vegetable, Shanghai: The salty preserved leafy tops of the large Chinese radish. The actual root vegetable is also pickled and used as a condiment or appetiser.
To store: Keeps indefinitely in refrigerator in glass container.

Preserved Vegetable, Szechual (jar choy): An indigenous speciality of Sichuan province in China, salted and flavoured with herbs and spices. It has a crisp texture and is usually sliced or shredded and cooked with pork, beef or chicken in soups and stir-fried dishes.
To store: In glass container indefinitely in the refrigerator.

Root Vegetables: Taro, Yam, Sweet Potato: These root vegetables are eaten as are potatoes anywhere else in the world. They are also grated and cooked to make crisp coatings on deep-fried savouries or sweets and ground to make flour for cooking.

Satay Sauce: Already prepared sauce imported from Malaysia or Singapore made from ground peanuts, oil and chillies.
To store: Keeps indefinitely in bottle.

Preserved Sausage (lup chiang): A tasty, sweet pork sausage smoked and faintly redolent of Chinese rice wine. They hang in pairs suspended by hooks in every Chinese grocery store and are popular in home cooking. They are placed to steam over the rice when it has almost completed its steaming stage.
To store: Wrap loosely in greaseproof paper and keep in refrigerator. They will keep up to three months.

Sesame Oil: A highly fragrant oil produced from sesame seeds. It has a delicately nutty flavour and is used as a flavouring agent and ingredient, but is never used as a cooking oil. Available in bottles.

Sesame Seeds: White small seeds from the sesame plant. Used for making sweets and as a garnish for many dishes.

Shark's Fins: Gelatinous whole dried shark's fins, very definitely a restaurant speciality as many long tedious hours have to be spent soaking, cleaning and preparing the fins. It is a gross breach of etiquette to leave any shark's fin soup in the bowl. It

the most prized of Chinese soups.

Sherry, Dry: A substitute for Chinese wine. A splash in some dishes adds just the right touch to complete the dish.
To store: Keeps indefinitely in bottle.

Shrimps, Dried: Tiny shelled shrimps that are preserved in salt and dried in the sun. They are an important ingredient particularly in home cooking and have a strong flavour so are used sparingly. They must be soaked 30 minutes in warm water and drained before use.
To store: In an airtight container.

Snake Beans (dow gwok): Very long round beans, hence the name. They have a stronger flavour than French beans and make interesting stir-fry dishes. The Sichuanese use them in a favourite dish with ground beef or shrimps.

Snow Peas (soot dow): Beautiful green pea pods eaten whole. They need only to be topped and tailed and stir-fried for a very short time. Also known as mange tout peas.

Spinach, Chinese (voor choy): A leafy green vegetable with a more delicate flavour than the English variety.

Spring Onions and Chives: Not strictly 'Chinese', but they are used so much in Chinese cooking, that they should be mentioned here.

Soy Sauce: Soy sauce is the best known of all Chinese sauces and is now an almost universal favourite. Made from fermented soy beans and allied with salt and wheat, it is the basic seasoning in Chinese cooking. It gives flavour and colour to cooked dishes and is also used as a 'dip' at the table. There are two soy sauces - *dark soy* sauce and *light soy*. The Chinese use the light soy more often than the dark as the flavour and texture of the lighter variety is more suitable for vegetables and soups, while the dark is good for heavier meat dishes, when a dark colour and heartier flavour is desired.
To store: Soy sauce in bottles keeps indefinitely at room temperature.

Sugars, Chinese: Malt sugar or maltose: Made from germinating barley in a process similar to making wine. It is similar to golden syrup, treacle or honey and these can be substituted.

Rock sugar: A crystallized sugar.

Slab Sugar: Produced from semi-refined brown sugar and has a 'caramelly' taste about it.
Substitute, soft brown sugar.

Turnip, Chinese (lor buk): Looks like an over-grown white carrot. It has a strong flavour and smell, but is very good in soups and some stir-fried dishes. Can also be grated to make savoury tidbits.

Turnip, Preserved (choong choy): Salted and preserved this is a valuable ingredient to the Chinese cook. It adds that little extra savoury flavour to some meat dishes (particularly minced meat) and soups. Possibly it is the Chinese equivalent to the Western bouillon cubes. I cannot recall ever seeing it written in any recipe book so it would seem that the Chinese feel they can go only far in 'educating' Westerners to our cooking.
To store: Remove to glass container, keeps indefinitely in the refrigerator.

Water Chestnuts (ma tai): These are bulb shaped stalks of a water plant and do not belong to the tree chestnut family. When fresh they have a brown outer skin covering a parchment white 'nut' which is juicy, sweet and very crisp. They add

delightful texture and interest to many dishes staying crisp even after long cooking. Sometimes they are available fresh in the Chinese shops and you should take advantage of them when you see them.
To store: Same as for bamboo shoots.

Watercress: Used in Chinese cooking quite a lot when in season and can also be bought in Chinese stores dried. Mostly used for soups.

Winter Vegetable (doong choy): Chopped, salted and preserved, this little vegetable adds a unique pungent flavour to many meat and fish dishes. Usually sold in attractive clay-pot jars, which make nice flower containers afterwards.
To store: In clay-pot indefinitely in the refrigerator.

Won Tons and Spring Roll Sheets: These can be made at home but to achieve a desired smooth finish they are more time consuming than many would believe. To purchase these ready made from a Chinese store is a lot easier, cheaper and a guarantee of fine quality.

Won Tons can be purchases either fresh or frozen and are locally made as well as imported. If the frozen variety are purchases. rewrap the unused portion in plastic and refreeze.

Spring roll sheets are imported from Hong Kong and Singapore and are of an excellent quality. They may be purchased in Chinese stores. Both are made from flour, eggs and water.

Vinegar, Chinese: There are at least four main types of Chinese vinegar, all made from fermented rice:
(I) *Black vinegar*: A strong, dark brown vinegar used mainly as a flavouring agent.
(II) *Red vinegar*: A clear, bright coloured vinegar favoured for seafood dishes. Used both for flavouring and as a condiment.
(III) *Sweet vinegar*: A black vinegar that is rather powerful even though it is sweet. Used for long cooked dishes such as braised or stewed dishes.
(IV) *White vinegar*: A white, rather mild vinegar similar to Western vinegar. Western vinegar is sharper and stronger.
(V) *Red sweet:* Preserved ginger slices pickled in a sweet syrup and coloured red.

Preserved Ginger: An attractive garnish for seafood dishes. Obtainable in jars.
To store: Keeps indefinitely in bottle.

The Chinese Kitchen

'Every family cooking pot has one black spot.'
Ancient Chinese Proverb

A carpenter must have his tools, an artist must have his brushes and so the cook who is both tradesman and artist, must have the right implements and utensils.

If you intend to do Chinese cooking at all well then you must equip yourself with the basic tools. To attempt to reproduce the works of art that the Chinese produce from their kitchens with anything short of these, is to invite gross inefficiency and frustration.

Happy news is that the Chinese kitchen lives unobtrusively in your own kitchen and can be accommodated entirely in the space of a small cupboard. Even better news is that, once you have invested in the right equipment, they will be your faithful servants for life! They ask very little of you, their utter simplicity of design makes them the easiest implements ever designed for cleaning.

Chinese cooking demands Chinese technique and Chinese technique demands tools that were created specifically for this. After all you don't play tennis with a ping pong bat, nor football with a golfball! So, if you want to bring a little bit of China into your home, start with the kitchen. Choose the same implements and utensils that the Chinese have used satisfactorily for many centuries. There is no valid reason for changing anything if it is good.

The Wok: The traditional rolled tempered steel wok responds well to changes of heat.

The curving, shallow bowl shape of the wok, makes it excellent for stir-frying, as the sloping sides facilitate the tossing and turning of ingredients essential for quick cooking. Deep-frying is efficient also, the wide area allows for great freedom in moving the foods in the oil and because of the rounded bottom much less oil is needed than in a more conventional deep fryer. Shallow-frying (such as for sausages, steaks, braising meats), steaming or boiling - the wok will happily cook anything from an egg to a chicken.

The rounded bottom has caused concern for some stoves especially electric plates and an iron ring frame can be used to support the wok more steadily, but better still, is a wok with a very slightly flattened bottom which entirely eliminates any wobbling. Be sure the flattened area at the base is only a few inches across and the inside of the wok is still smoothly rounded. Woks featuring a wide flat bottom are really glorified English frying pans and will not perform efficiently for Chinese cooking. You should select woks made only by Chinese for Chinese.

To season your Wok: Wash your wok in warm soapy water and dry well. Put on to a very low heat and rub the surface with a cloth pad impregnated with oil. Continue to rub while heating until the pad comes out clean. Wash and dry again, rubbing a little oil on the surface each time before putting away. It is a good idea to soak the wok in warm soapy water immediately after use if you cannot wash it immediately; any food burnt on to the surface will then lift off easily with a cloth. Steel wool and Velvet soap will not harm your wok. Just make sure it is dry before putting it away. Your wok will darken with age and use, don't worry, a black wok is the proud hallmark of a good cook!

Wok Spatula: The right companion for your wok is the Chinese spatula, literally known by the Chinese as the wok shovel. This is curved to fit exactly the sloping sides of the wok and possesses surprising strength. It is inexpensive and a great joy to use. Spatulas made from iron or stainless steel are practical but you must be sure to thoroughly dry the iron spatula before putting it away.

Wok Lid: Also necessary is a lid to sit below the rim of the wok. This lid is dome-shaped and allows for maximum circulation of steam. The lid is important for cooking vegetables and simmering meats.

Strainer or Skimmer: An essential accessory especially for lifting foods deep-fried in oil and for straining hot liquids. The long handle protects your hand from hot steam and burning oils. The new stainless steel strainers are perhaps not quite as decorative as the old-fashioned wire skimmers, but they are easy to clean.

Chinese Chopper: Absolutely your best friend in a Chinese kitchen. Life for one day without the chopper is a day fraught with frustration and despair. The Chinese chopper may look fearsomely wicked, but overcome your initial reluctance and with a little practice, you will become so attached to it, you will forget your other kitchen knives. They come in various widths and weights - ideally, you should have two, one for fine slicing and one for chopping through bones. However, an all purpose size Number 3, will suffice the average cook. Usually made of carbon steel, you should keep it sharp the same way you sharpen your other knives. The Chinese chopper slices vegetables, minces meat, chops through poultry bones, guts and scales fish, crushes garlic, picks up food from the chopping board and carries it to the wok, sharpens pencils, digs and prunes in the garden. No wonder life is impossible without the faithful chopper!

Chopping Board: The traditional Chinese chopping board is a level cross-section of a tree trunk. This board is still favoured by the Chinese, particularly in restaurants, as a large one is so heavy it will not move during chopping. It is also kinder to the blades of the chopper. Most modern homes however, find it a little tedious to maintain and wash, as it should never be submerged in water. A sturdy wooden board or the polyurethane boards are adequate. Never use a slippery surfaced cutting board on which your food will slip and slide and which will also blunt your knife.

Bamboo Steamer: The food is put on a dish inside this steamer basket with bamboo lid on top and placed over boiling water in the wok to steam. Bamboo minimises condensation as it is porous. The baskets are especially suitable for steaming buns and dim sims. The steamers come in layers and can be stacked one on top of the other with one lid.

Apart from the many steamed dishes in the Chinese cuisine, such as fish and minced meats, steaming is an excellent way of re-heating cold food. Steamers should be at least 5 cm (2 inches) smaller in diameter than your wok. A practical substitute for a bamboo steamer is a cake rack or two wooden or bamboo crossed sticks. These form a platform on which to place your dish of food. Place in your wok, add a little water and cover with wok lid. You could lightly cover the food with foil to reduce condensation if you don't have a bamboo lid.

Easi-grip: A marvellously efficient device for picking up and taking hot dishes to the table. This utensil is indispensable in the kitchen especially for removing dishes that have been steamed. Steam burns can be very painful. The esi-grip eliminates the clumsy use of oven mitts.

Chopsticks: (For preparing - bamboo or wooden). Truly an extension of your own hand. Chopsticks are versatile as the wok, they stir, beat, whisk, pick up, turn over and separate foods in the wok. Replaces a half dozen or so other utensils.

Chopsticks for the Table: They come in bamboo, lacquered wood, bone, ivory and in lavish days-gone-by jade, agate, gold and silver. Bamboo chopsticks are the easiest to use, but they are considered unrefined for company. Ivory is favoured in high society and like silver cutlery, ten pairs of ivory chopsticks make a very acceptable wedding gift. Since there are no knives set at the Chinese table, all food is cut into bite-size portions beforehand in the kitchen; chopsticks enable individual pieces of food to be taken to the mouth with a delicate amount of coating sauce; eating mouthfuls of sauce picked up with forks and spoons unbalances flavours intended by the cook. Rice however, is not picked up with chopsticks, but pushed in, or rather shovelled in, as daintily as the action makes possible. This is normal practice to Chinese, but somewhat unacceptable to non-Chinese.

For twenty years I witnessed the painful attempts of my students to pick up a few rice grains at a time from bowl to mouth, but I have dismally failed with the exception of a few valiant ones to change their ways. Emily Post continues to have her way. Foreigners can take heart that Chinese too have to learn how to use chopsticks. Granted, we start our learning and practising from a very young age, but like handwriting, chopstick holding does vary a great deal in spite of the classic method taught at the beginning. The best advice to anyone wishing to learn, is to practice as often as you can; reading about it will really not help very much except to start you off. Try to think chopsticks as your own fingers. If you feel you look a little different, don't worry too much, if it feels quite comfortable and you are managing at all, then that is all that matters.

Porcelain Spoon: We do not enjoy sipping soups with metal spoons that become heated and scald the tongue. A porcelain spoon is used by the Chinese cook to measure one tablespoon and as a 'taster', it adds no metal flavour to foods.

Cooking Methods

'One must never disgrace oneself by serving a dish that is over-cooked, under-cooked, crookedly cut, or deficient in seasoning.'
Confucius 'On an essay on morality'

Cooking Chinese food calls for unfamiliar techniques, but with a little practice and patience, you will find it reasonably simple.

Stir-frying (chow): The fastest way of cooking ingredients that have been cut into even bite-size portions; this method often takes less than one minute and seldom more than three. A small amount of oil is heated in the wok ad the food is constantly stirred and tossed around until done. Sometimes (in the case of vegetables) a small amount of liquid is added after the initial stir-frying. The wok is covered with a lid enabling the food to be cooked in its own juice.

In stir-frying, the heat of the wok is critical. This is what the Chinese call correct 'wok hay'. It is a good cook who really understands 'wok hay'. You must learn to toss and turn the foods to be sitr-fried quickly, so that they will not burn, but will acquire a light 'glazing' of hot oil that ensures the flavours and juices are locked inside the ingredient being cooked.

You have to realize that even after a small amount of liquid (either water or chicken stock) is added to the wok and the lid placed on the heat is still at maximum point. There is the Western tendency to turn the heat down at this point to low and 'stew' the meat and vegetables.

Plunging: This is the alternative method to stir-frying of cooking green vegetables. In this plunging method, the vegetables are sliced first, then added to a pot of rapidly boiling water in which a little salt has been added. Naturally, there is enough water to cover the vegetables. Keep on maximum heat until the water returns to the boil, then time the vegetables as directed in the recipe. Most vegetables take from 1-2 minutes on the boil. Very rarely do they take longer.

Immediately strain the vegetables, and place under cold running water. This arrests and further cooking action. Drain very thoroughly and place on a plate. They need now only to be combined or 'married' with the meat in the wok.

There is much to recommend this method as it simplifies procedures for the busy hostess. The 'plunging' can be done several hours earlier and the final cooking is only a matter of heating and combining the vegetables with the other ingredients in the wok. I mostly use this method when entertaining.

For everyday cooking, I stir-fry my vegetables because there is absolutely no waste of flavour and nutrient; what goes into the wok, comes out, everything is eaten, even the liquid. In the plunging method, nutrients are lost in the water which goes down the sink. If you continue to boil vegetables and throw away the water, then you will end up with the healthiest sink in town!

Steaming (jing): The food is placed in a dish or plate suspended above water usually in a wok and steamed until done. The dish can also be placed in a special bamboo steamer. Fish and minced meat dishes cook particularly well this way; flavours are added to the food before steaming and the dish is brought from the steamer straight to the table. A method which brings out purity of taste and recommended for the health conscious.

If you do not have a wok (shame on you though!) and you are looking for an alternative way of steaming food, voila!

Place a wire rack in an electric frypan, put about 2.5 cm (1 inch) of boiling water in the bottom of the pan and place your plate holding the food on the rack. Just be sure there is not much water that it will touch the food while it is cooking. Cover the pan with the lid with the vent open. Maintain a gentle steady steam (usually about 150ºC 300ºF) keeps the water simmering).

If you are steaming fish in an electric frypan, be sure the temperature is not so high that the water is crating too vigorous a steam. The delicate flesh of fish could disintegrate from too much and too long a steaming.

Fricasseeing (mun): The ingredients are first lightly fried in a little oil until browned, then simmered in water or stock until done. Closely allied to stewing.

Red Cooking (hoong sieu): The same method as in 'mun' but the simmering is done in a sauce made up largely of soy sauce.

Deep-frying (ja-ah): Enough hot oil is used to completely cover the food so that it is crispy-golden on the outside and thoroughly cooked but tender on the inside.

Roasting, Barbecuing (sieu): Meat is first seasoned, then placed on a rack in the oven or upon a spit over direct heat. Meat is never placed in a pan to roast but is always free standing, with heat circulating evenly around all sides. Usually there is a pan on the bottom of the oven to catch marinating juices.

Shallow Frying (dien): With aluminium of movement in a small amount of oil. Often a sauce is added to complete the cooking process. Whole fish is often cooked in this way.

Crack Pot Method (dunn): Ingredients are placed in a container with a tight fitting lid and the container placed inside a larger pot of water to steam. Usually a long process and favoured for cooking 'big' soups such as winter melon soup and chicken and wine soup.

Whichever method you are going to use, I cannot over stress the necessity to thoroughly prepare the ingredients and have them neatly assembled on the bench within easy reach before you begin any cooking. Otherwise, your cooking will be punctuated with shouts of 'who has taken the celery' and 'where's the cornflour?'.

If you want to enjoy your Chinese cooking, then follow these guidelines before you commence any cooking. Meats should be sliced, marinated and set aside in a bowl, with accompanying spices such as ginger or garlic if used; vegetables should be washed, sliced and placed in neat individual piles on one plate; dried ingredients such as mushrooms or cloud ear fungus should be soaked twice in warm water, first time for rinsing. After the prescribed time of soaking, drain, squeeze out excess moisture and place them with the vegetables.

Listed seasoning should be mixed in a bowl nearby; cornflour thickening should be mixed in a small bowl nearby; peanut oil, soy sauce, Chinese Rice Wine, sugar, salt, pepper and cornflour should be on a try nearby.

'Marrying Ingredients': It is often said that Chinese cooking is a beautiful 'marriage' of flavours. When I instruct my students to 'marry' the food, I am referring to the method of quickly turning and tossing the ingredients together so that they combine to join up with each other to make one harmonious blend.

Rice and Noodles

'A meal without rice is like a beautiful girl with only one eye.'
Old Chinese Saying

Rice is so important in the Chinese daily diet that to signify dinner is ready, one can simply say 'The rice pot is open.' When I was a little girl and I would ask, as all children do, 'What's for dinner?' the short and succinct reply was always 'Rice, what else?'

To the Chinese, rice is life, it is 'the sweat of man's brow' and not to be wasted. To encourage children to respect this view, they are warned that they will marry a pockmarked man or woman one day, if they leave any rice grains behind in their bowls. Obviously, a real concern, where smallpox once left its mark on so many.

There are many such stories surrounding rice; to upset a bowl of rice means bad luck and to be down to 'the shirt on one's back' in English, is the same as the term 'begging for rice'. To lose one's job is to say that 'the rice bowl is broken'.

Rice is very easily digested, and may account for the fact that the Chinese eat such vast quantities and don't appear to put on the weight one would expect. It may also account for the rather tiresome complaint that Chinese food leaves one feeling hungry a little while after a full meal. Heavy foods such as dairy products and red meats sit on the stomach, so the Westerner is accustomed to a 'full' feeling.

The Chinese say there are 7000 varieties of rice, incredible as that seems and I sometimes think there are almost as many methods of cooking rice as there are varieties. It would seem sensible to me that if China's one thousand million people have been sustained for countless centuries by rice then they should know how to cook it.

Steamed Rice
The Absorption Method

Properly cooked rice is an absolute necessity to your Chinese cooking skills, and must be your starting point.

You will need:
Desired quantity of long or short grain rice. Allow ½ cup per person; 1 cup for each Chinese friend. Rice doubles in volume when cooked.

Preparation:
1. Place rice in a saucepan and wash in cold water. Swill rice around saucepan in a circular movement until the water becomes cloudy and milky
2. Rinse, add more water and repeat until water is clear.
3. Cover rice with 1 cm (½ inch) water above level of rice. Cover with lid.

Cooking:
1. Bring the rice to a rapid boil over high heat. When the water starts to bubble over, reduce heat only enough to arrest it.
2. Continue on medium heat until water is absorbed. The rice is still moist with little 'craters' but there must not be any loose water in the pot before you reduce the heat to a low simmer. You may stir the rice just before turning down the heat. Simmer now for 15-20 minutes. Longer simmering will not harm the rice, but you will probably get a light crust on the bottom of the pot.
This fine layer of 'crust' is quite normal especially if you are cooking a fairly large amount of rice, as the simmering can be extended to a longer period of time. This simmering period is the actual cooking process needed in order to cook each grain through to perfection.

> *Points of interest:*
> No salt is added to Chinese steamed rice. The saucepan is tightly covered with a lid throughout the cooking time, locking in the steam. Because the water has been absorbed, the rice is steamed rather than boiled.
>
> The Chinese believe undercooked rice causes indigestion and gives rise to a number of other ailments. When properly cooked, the grains should be tender and not gluggy.
>
> The crust on the bottom of the saucepan is an indication that the rice has had the proper steaming time. The crust should be a light golden colour and is enjoyed with some hot soup (or even hot water) poured over it. Otherwise, simply soak the pot for a short while. The crust will easily lift off and, after straining, can be added to leftover rice to make fried rice.

Cantonese Fried Rice

You will need:
500 g (1 lb) cooked white rice
125 g (4 oz) Chinese roast pork or thick bacon or ham
125 g (4 oz) shrimps
1 cup bean sprouts
2 stalks spring onions, chopped
2 eggs lightly beaten with a little salt
4 tablespoons oil

Seasoning:
Salt to taste
1 tablespoon light soy sauce
1/2 tablespoon dark soy sauce

Preparation:
1. Blanch the shrimps in boiling water for 20 seconds.

Cooking:
1. Heat the wok, add 1 tablespoon oil and pour in the eggs and cook until they are just beginning to softly set (about 1 minute). Remove and set aside.
2. Add the remaining oil, stir-fry shrimps, bacon or roast pork and spring onions for a minute or two. Add rice, working it well into the heat of the wok with the Chinese spatula and combining well with all the other ingredients. Continue turning and pressing the rice into the sides of the wok for another two minutes. Make sure you break down any lumps in the rice.
3. Add bean sprouts, then return the cooked eggs to the rice, breaking them into small pieces with the spatula, add the soy sauces and serve (a little extra chopped spring onions will add fresh colour). Salt to taste.

Alternative method for cooking eggs:
Oil a flat frying pan and when hot, pour in a little egg mixture to make a thin pancake. Repeat until the eggs are used up. Lay the egg pancakes on to a board and slice into thin julienne strips.

Note: Fried rice is best made from rice cooked the day before.

Jook
(The Chinese Breakfast)

This is a favourite Chinese breakfast made from rice that bears little resemblance in appearance and flavour to the Western sweet porridge of oats. It is more like a thick rice soup and we call it jook. Foreigners call it congee, why I don't know.

You will need:
1 cup short grain rice
2.5 litres (10 cups) chicken stock
A little salt
Peanut oil

Mix together:
315 g (10 oz) minces pork or minced rump or topside beef
1 cup spring onions, finely chopped
1 cup water chestnuts, finely chopped
1 teaspoon salt
1 teaspoon light soy sauce

Condiments:
Bowl of chopped spring onions
Small bowl of sweet cucumbers (char gwar)
Small bowl of Sichuan preserved vegetables, (jar coy) optional
Small bowl finely shredded ginger
1 cup roasted peanuts, optional
Dark soy sauce with a few drops of sesame oil

Preparation:
1. Wash the rice in a small pot, drain off water, then work in with your fingers a little salt and peanut oil. Stand for one hour.

Cooking:
1. Bring the stock to boil, add the rice, stirring until it comes back to the boils. Reduce heat and simmer 2-3 hours. In that time the rice completely breaks down and the jook has become thick and creamy.
2. Beat in the minced pork or beef mixture (or you can make little pork balls, see recipe for pork ball soup). Cook a further 5 minutes.
3. Adjust salt to taste.
4. Ladle into individual bowls. Each person adds their own favourite condiments.

Hainan Chicken Rice

You will need:
1 roasting chicken, approximately 1.5 kg (3 lb)
5 cloves garlic, slap lightly with broad side of chopper to remove outer skin, but don't break the flesh of the garlic
2 by 5 mm (¼ inch) slices ginger
2½ cups rice
125 ml (½ cup) chicken fat removed from the chicken. Make up quantity with a little peanut oil if not quite enough. I make a habit of saving the pads of fat from the chicken and deep freezing them. They really do add tremendous flavour to stir-fried vegetables and omelettes, but from a health point of view I do feel a wee bit guilty using too much animal fat.

Dips for the chicken:

Chilli Dip: mix together
2 teaspoons chilli sauce or Tabasco
2 teaspoons finely minced ginger
1 teaspoon minced garlic
Squeeze of lemon or lime juice
 all over and mix

Ginger Dip: mix together
1 tablespoon finely shredded ginger
1 tablespoon shredded spring onions
2 tablespoons salad oil
Dash salt and pepper

Dark Soy Dip:
Dark black soy sauce, a special sauce
 of Malaysia and Indonesia

Light Soy Dip:
Light soy sauce mixed with
 half quantity of sesame oil

Preparation:
1. Clean the chicken well inside and outside. Remove the fat pads and keep. Rub some salt on the outside of the chicken and stand 10 minutes. (This prevents the skin from breaking during cooking.)
2. Place the chicken in a saucepan and cover with cold water. Add 1 teaspoon salt. Cook quickly until boiling and maintain boil for 5 minutes. Turn the chicken over to the other side and cook another 5 minutes. Turn off the heat and let the chicken stand for 30 minutes, then remove from pot.
3. Wash the rice in the normal manner, draining off all water.
4. Chop the chicken in Chinese fashion and arrange on a serving plate.
5. Chop the chicken fat into shreds and arrange with garlic and ginger and washed rice.

Cooking:
1. In a hot wok, heat the chicken fat shreds and fry until the fat has melted. Remove remains of the fat, then add garlic and ginger and gently saute 1-2 minutes. Be careful you don't burn the garlic! Remove and put aside. Add washed rice to the wok, turn up the heat, and stir-fry over high heat for 2 minutes. Remove rice to saucepan ready for cooking.
2. Pour enough chicken broth to cover the rice 2 cm above the level of the rice. Add the garlic and 1 slice of ginger to the rice pot and cook in the normal absorption method (see earlier recipe for cooking rice).
3. Serve bowls of chicken rice accompanied by a bowl of clear chicken soup together with a serving of chopped chicken and various dips.

Noodle Salad

This recipe is simple to prepare yet is delicious and represents the best of good food. Serve the salad on a bed of lettuce surrounded with sliced tomatoes as an unusual side dish - most refreshing on a warm day!

You will need:
175 g (6 oz) bean thread noodles
1 tablespoon oil (preferably groundnut)
2 teaspoons salt
350 g (12 oz) bean sprouts
6 spring onions, finely shredded
1½ teaspoons chilli bean sauce
1½ tablespoons white rice vinegar
1 tablespoon light soy sauce
2 teaspoons sesame oil

Preparation:
1. Soak the noodles in a large bowl of warm water for 5 minutes. (While they are soaking, prepare the other ingredients.) When the noodles are soft, drain them well and cut them into 7.5 cm (3 inch) lengths using scissors or a knife.
2. Heat a wok or large frying-pan and add the oil, salt, bean sprouts and spring onions. Stir-fry for 10 seconds, then add the chilli bean sauce, rice vinegar, soy sauce, sesame oil and noodles and cook for 1 minute. Allow the mixture to cool, then refrigerate.
3. Serve cold as an accompaniment to grilled or cold meats.

Hokkien Noodles with a Spicy Beef Sauce - page 35

Won Ton in Chicken
Soup - page 39

Seafood and Spinach Soup - page 43

**Imperial Prawns -
A Palace Dish - page 53**

Combination Fried Noodles

You will need:
1 pkt egg noodles, called 'chow mien' noodles
125 g chicken meat, uncooked
125 g green prawns, deveined and washed
125 g Chinese roast pork, available at Chinese restaurants or deli
2 cups Chinese cabbage, Bok choy, Choi sum or Chinese broccoli
1 cup celery, diagonally sliced
6 Chinese dried mushrooms, soaked 45 minutes, rinsed and sliced
1/2 cup bamboo shoots - sliced
2 tablespoons light soy sauce

Seasoning: Mix in a bowl:
1 teaspoon cornflour
1/2 teaspoon salt
1/2 teaspoon sugar
1 tablespoon light soy sauce
1 tablespoon Chinese (Shaohsing) rice wine
1 teaspoon sesame oil
1/2 cup chicken stock
Peanut oil

Preparation:
1. Pour a kettle of boiling water over the noodles in a bowl or pot, and stand 3-4 minutes. Gently swirl the noodles around to loosen, strain off the water, and spread the noodles out on a tray to dry.
2. Slice the chicken into small bite-sized portions, and sprinkle with a little light soy sauce, wine and a light dusting of cornflour.
3. Cut the prawns into halves if very large, and slice roast pork.

Cooking:
1. Add 3 tablespoons peanut oil to a pre-heated wok, swirling around the sides to coat the surface. When the oil begins to smoke, add the noodles in the shape of a 'cake', and reduce the heat to moderate to fry the noodles until the bottom of the noodles begins to crisp and turn golden brown in sections. Turn the noodles over to crisp and brown in several sections. (You might want to fry the noodles in two separate batches.) When noodles are hot all the way through, remove to the oven to keep warm.
2. Add 2 tablespoons oil to the wok and when smoking, stir-fry chicken for a minute before adding the prawns. Continue to cook over high heat until the meats are cooked (about 1-2 minutes), add mushrooms and bamboo shoots to combine quickly for a few seconds more. Remove the contents to a plate.
3. Add a little more oil and when hot, add the vegetables to toss until glazed. Add a little water to create some steam (about 1/4 cup), cover with the wok lid, and continue to cook over high heat for 2 minutes. Return the chicken and prawns contents, stir in the seasoning, and when the sauce is lightly thickened, finally toss in the Chinese roast pork to combine.

    Serve over fried noodles.

Singapore Noodles

Ingredients:
Rice vermicelli (Mai fun) or Rice Sticks (fine) approx. 200 g
1 small onion, sliced
3 tablespoons carrots, finely julienned
2 tablespoons green capsicum, finely julienned
1/2 cup cook prawns
2 tablespoons red capsicum, finely julienned
2 eggs, lightly beaten
1/2 cup Chinese Roast Pork (Char Siew)
1 cup bean sprouts

Seasoning:
2 tablespoons curry powder or paste
1/2 teaspoon salt
Splash light soy sauce

Garnish:
Sprinkling fried shallots, available in Asian stores
Chopped spring onions

Cooking:
1. Soak the rice vermicelli in hot water for 3-4 minutes, drain and rinse.
2. Heat a little peanut oil in the wok, pour in half of the beaten egg, and make an egg 'pancake'. Remove and slice finely.
3. Add 3 tablespoons oil to the wok and when just smoking, pour in the remaining beaten egg. Scramble until softly set, then push to the sides of the wok, add the carrots, capsicum and onions to stir fry for 1 minute. Add the roast pork slices, prawns and bean sprouts, combine quickly while stirring in the seasoning.
4. Finally, add the rice vermicelli to the wok, tossing and tumbling all the ingredients until everything is well combined.

Serve garnished with fried onions and chopped spring onions.

Hokkien Noodles with a Spicy Beef Sauce

Ingredients:
300 g (1 packet) fresh Hokkien noodles, available at Asian stores
2 teaspoons sesame oil
250 g good quality minced beef
Peanut oil

Seasoning for Beef: Mix in a bowl:
2 teaspoons light soy sauce
1/2 teaspoon sugar
Splash Chinese (Shaohsing) rice wine
2 teaspoons cornflour

In each of the four serving bowls, add the following:
1 teaspoon chopped spring onions
1/2 teaspoon chilli bean paste, available at Asian stores
1 teaspoon vinegar
1 teaspoon dark soy sauce
1 teaspoon fish sauce
2 tablespoons chicken stock

Garnishing:
Handful of chopped spring onions and/or fresh coriander

Cooking:
1. *The beef sauce*:   Heat 3 tablespoons peanut oil in a pre-heated wok or pan and stir-fry the beef mince with the minced garlic until the colour changes - aproximately 1-2 minutes. Mix in the seasoning.
2. *The noodles*: Place the noodles into a large bowl, and cover with boiling water. Stir, and allow to stand 3-4 minutes before draining. Rinse briefly, then stir in sesame oil.
3. *To serve*: Place a large handful of the noodles over the ingredients in each bowl, top with the cooked meat mixture and garnish with a little extra chopped spring onions and/or fresh coriander.

Just before eating, stir the noodles in your bowl to combine all the ingredients well.

Fresh Noodles with Three Kinds of Mushrooms

You will need:
1 pkt (170 g) fresh egg noodles, available in Chinese stores
6 Chinese dried mushrooms, soaked in warm water 45 minutes, water squeezed out and julienned
1/4 cup straw mushrooms, cut each into halves
6 canned abalone mushrooms, julienned
3/4 cup spring onions or chives, shredded (use mainly white parts)
2 tablespoons oil

Seasoning:
1 tablespoon light soy sauce
1 tablespoon oyster sauce
Pinch salt and pepper
1/4 cup chicken stock

Garnish:
Fresh coriander

Cooking:
1. Blanch noodles in a pot of boiling water for 1 minute until 'al dente'. Drain rinse briefly and keep warm.
2. Heat 2 tablespoons oil in a pre-heated wok or pan and stir-fry all the mushrooms together with the spring onions for 1 minute, add seasoning simmer another minute.
3. Add the noodles into the wok to combine with the mushrooms, stirring quickly over high heat.

Soups

Soup is regarded as a beverage to wash down rice and other foods and is therefore served throughout the entire meal.

I make a habit of collecting unused chicken carcasses, necks, giblets and wings and freezing them. It is not long before I have enough material for making a good pot of stock, which I then freeze in small containers.

Chicken Stock
(makes 2.5 litres or 10 cups)

You will need:
1 chicken, approximately 1.5 kg (3 lb) or the equivalent in chicken pieces or bones
1 pork bone or pork chop (optional)
1 piece fresh ginger, size of small walnut
1 stalk spring onion
1 teaspoon salt
Water to cover the chicken

Preparation:
1. Wash the chicken thoroughly and pat dry with a paper towel. Lightly rub the chicken skin with a little salt. This prevents the skin from breaking.
2. Lightly bruise (flatten) ginger with flat surface of chopper.
3. Lightly bruise stalk of spring onion.
4. Place ginger and spring onion in the cavity of the chicken and place in a saucepan with cold water to cover. Add 1 teaspoon salt.

Cooking:
1. Bring to the boil and cook for 8 minutes. Turn chicken on to its back and boil for another 8 minutes. Turn off the heat and skim stock. Let chicken stand in stock for at least 1 hour, then remove. Skim stock again.
2. Bring the stock to the boil again with the pork bones (if using), skim again, then simmer a further 30 minutes. Remove meat bones, cool and strain.

Pork Stock

Follow the Chicken Stock recipe using 1 kg (2 lb) of pork bones and 250 g (8 oz) or pork meat.

Chicken, Shrimp and Mushroom Soup

You will need:
1.5 litres (6 cups) chicken stock
1/2 teaspoon salt, dash white pepper
1/2 teaspoon finely minced ginger
1 cup sliced chicken fillet
1/2 cup fresh shrimps or prawns
6 medium Chinese dried mushrooms, soaked 30 minutes, stalks removed and sliced
1/2 cup bamboo shoots, sliced into julienne strips
2 eggs, lightly beaten
1 tablespoon Chinese (Shaohsing) rice wine
1 cup chopped spring onions

Thickening:
3 tablespoons cornflour dissolved in 3 tablespoons water.

Preparation:
1. Assemble all the ingredients on one plate. Have eggs and thickening nearby.
2. Cut prawns into bite-size pieces if large.

Cooking:
1. Combine the chicken stock, salt, pepper and ginger with mushrooms and bamboo shoots. Simmer together for 5 minutes. Add the chicken and shrimps and simmer for another 3 minutes.
2. Stir in the cornflour thickening until the soup begins to boil again and thickens. Taste for extra salt if needed. Turn off heat and slowly add eggs, gently stirring for about half a minute. Add sherry and serve in a large soup tureen, garnished with chopped spring onions.

Won Ton in Chicken Soup

Won tons are little dumplings filled with pork or prawns and are enjoyed in a bowl of clear chicken soup. Sometimes they are deep-fried and make terrific party food. They are made from very thin noodle pastry dough, which is readily available in Chinese stores.

'Won' means cloud and 'ton' means swallow, since won ton wrappers are so light and agile, the experience is like swallowing clouds! Chinese poetic licence, but then why not? They are guaranteed to bring Chinese out of hiding any time.

You will need:
1 packet won ton skins, approximately 80 = 250 g (8 oz)
Filling:
125 g (4 oz) minced pork
125 g (4 oz) fresh green prawns
1/2 cup finely chopped water chestnuts
6 Chinese dried mushrooms, soaked 1 hour, stalks removed and finely chopped
2 teaspoons dried shrimps, soaked 30 minutes and finely chopped
1 cup finely chopped spring onions
A small amount of egg, lightly beaten
2 teaspoons salt
1/2 teaspoon pepper
2 litres (8 cups) chicken soup, strained of any impurities

Preparation:
1. Devein and wash the prawns, then mince with chopper. Mix in a bowl with minced pork, mushrooms, dried shrimps, water chestnuts, spring onions, egg and seasoning.
2. Lay one square on the palm of your hand. Place 1/2 teaspoon of filling in top corner of skin half way down. Fold over to seal, then twist bottom right corner to meet back of left corner and press to seal. (You may need a little water to seal.)

Cooking:
1. Heat chicken soup, with 2 slices of fresh ginger and salt to taste.
2. Bring a pot of water to the boil. Add won tons and cook until they 'float', approximately 2 minutes. Remove them with a skimmer or slotted spoon and transfer to individual soup bowls.
3. Ladle boiling chicken broth over the won tons, sprinkle in a little light soy sauce and sesame oil and garnish with chopped spring onions.

> *Points of interest*:
> Sometimes we include a few slices of Chinese roast pork or chicken pieces in the soup to make a more substantial snack. Although I have included this in the soup section, won tons are not really part of a meal. Won tons are eaten as a snack meal to be enjoyed at any time other than at a regular meal time. A full house is guaranteed whenever won ton soup is on the menu!

Beef and Chinese Turnip Soup

You will need:
500 g (1 lb) gravy beef (shin or beef) or beef flank
3 slices ginger
1 teaspoon dried shrimps, lightly rinsed in warm water
500 g (1 lb) turnips. Chinese turnips are good (lor buk) but English ones will do
2 tablespoons chopped spring onions
1 tablespoon brandy
Salt to taste

Preparation:
1. Cut beef into bite-size chunks.
2. Peel and cut turnips into bite-size chunks.

Cooking:
1. Simmer beef, ginger and dried shrimps in 2.5 litres (10 cups) of cold water for one hour.
2. Add turnips to the beef broth and simmer a further 30 minutes.
3. Add salt to taste (approximately 1 1/2 teaspoons), then brandy (especially good in winter) just before serving. Serve garnished with chopped spring onions.

> *Points of interest*:
> A deliciously simple soup which can be made and served up confidently to Chinese friends. Try beetroot instead of turnip for a change.

Chinese Cabbage and Bean Curd Soup

You will need:
1.5 litres (6 cups) chicken stock
3 slices ginger
1/2 head small Chinese cabbage (wong buk or gai choy)

Preparation:
1. Wash and cut cabbage across into 2.5 cm (1 inch) sections.
2. Cut bean curd squares into quarters.

Cooking:
1. Add ginger slices to stock and simmer 5 minutes. Add cabbage, simmer 3 minutes. Add cabbage, simmer 3 minutes, then add bean curds for another 3 minutes.
2. Add salt to taste, serve in a soup tureen, and sprinkle in sesame oil.

Noodle Soup

Noodles are as much of a favourite with Chinese as spaghetti is with the Italians, but they are enjoyed more as a snack food than anything else. Lunch time, supper time, even breakfast can be a good time for noodles and they nearly always appear at birthday parties, when they signify longevity.

Chinese stores carry a good supply of all kinds of noodles, both the dried packaged varieties (of which there are many) and fresh noodles (egg noodles and rice noodles). Any of these can be prepared in either stir-fried noodle dishes or in soup.

You will need:
2.5 litres (10 cups) of chicken broth, as in won ton soup
250 g (8 oz) egg or rice noodles
4 Chinese dried mushrooms, soaked 30 minutes, stems discarded and cut into halves
2 stalks spring onions, sliced finely
2 cups Chinese cabbage cut into julienne strips, washes and leaves roughly broken into halves
250 g (8 oz) Chinese roast pork (char sieu) thinly sliced, or chicken or pork fillet
4 tablespoons peanut oil

Seasoning:
1 tablespoon light soy sauce
1 teaspoon salt
1 teaspoon sesame oil
½ teaspoon chilli sauce if desired

Preparation :
1. Bring a pot of water to the boil, add noodles and cook for 2 minutes. (There are some noodles that might take a little longer, but be sure not to overcook them. They should be soft on the outside, but still firm in the centre - what the Italians call 'al dente'.) Drain, rinse in cold water and gently stir in 2 tablespoons of peanut oil.

Cooking :
1. Heat the wok, add 2 tablespoons of oil and when slightly smoking, stir-fry chicken or pork slices, mushrooms, spring onions and cabbage for 2 minutes. Add roast pork and seasoning to remove.
2. Bring chicken broth to the boil, add noodles to cook until soup is boiling again. Ladle noodles into individual soup bowls with the chicken broth and arrange stir-fried ingredients on top. Some extra fresh spring onion slices should be added as a fresh garnish.

> *Points of interest:*
> Chinese roast pork is available ready cooked in many Chinese stores, or from Chinese restaurants. Fresh pork or chicken fillet could be used as an alternative to roast pork, in which case, the meat is thinly sliced and stir-fried with the mushrooms.

Fish Soup

This recipe was given to me by my fourth uncle as a very special favour, a rare privilege, as he guarded his recipes like precious jewels not to be given away carelessly. It is one of my true favourites, but apart from this the soup is chock-full of goodness. Chicken broth is, as everyone knows, restorative and there are all the other wonderful fresh ingredients to go with it, fish, eggs and the noodles; made from the starch of the mung bean. It is an ideal soup for anyone recuperating from illness, for not only is it nourishing, light and digestible, but stimulating in its delicate flavour.

You will need:
1.5 litres (6 cups) chicken stock
2 fillets flathead fish, approximately 500 g (1 lb)
½ teaspoon minced ginger
30 g (1 oz) cellophane noodles
2 eggs, lightly beaten
Small teaspoon salt, dash white pepper
3 tablespoons cornflour dissolved in 3 tablespoons chicken stock
2 slices smoked ham, finely minced.

Note: Chicken stock must be first grade, sweet and clear of 'blemishes'. Eggs added into Chinese soups must never be over cooked or else they will harden. They are stirred in 'off the heat' so that the tendrils float like flowers.

Preparation:
1. Scrape the fish meat away from the skin and bones with a metal spoon. Mince finely with chopper or in a food processor. Place on a plate with the minced ginger.
2. Assemble seasoning, eggs, thickening and ham garnish nearby.
3. Heat 1 litre (4 cups) of oil in the wok until just smoking. Reduce heat. Separate noodles and deep-fry a little at a time. Noodles will immediately puff up. Flip quickly on to other side for another second or two. Remove and drain on a paper towel.

Cooking:
1. Heat the chicken stock, adding fish mince (with the teaspoon minced ginger) a little at a time, beating with chopsticks or fork to separate. It is a good idea to remove the saucepan from the heat while adding the fish, otherwise the fish could 'lump'.
2. Add the cornflour thickening and stir until soup comes to the boil again and thickens. Consistency should be smooth and velvety.
3. Season with salt and pepper. Turn off the heat, then slowly add eggs, gently stirring for about half a minute.
4. Serve in a large soup tureen, drop deep-fried cellophane noodles into the centre and garnish with minced ham on top.

Winter Melon Soup

This soup is much favoured at Chinese dinner parties, the delicately flavoured melon flesh combines beautifully with the ham and chicken broth.

You will need:
1.5 litres (6 cups) chicken stock
8 Chinese dried mushrooms, soaked 30 minutes, stalks discarded and shredded
500 g (1 lb) winter melon or other melons in season
1 rasher smoked ham about 5 mm (1/4 inch) thick by 15 cm (6 inches) long

Preparation :
1. Peel the melon, discarding skin and seeds. Cut the melon into 5 mm (1/4 inch) thick slices, then cut into 4 cm (1 1/2 inch) pieces.
2. Cut smoked ham in approximately the same sizes.

Cooking :
1. Add sliced melon and mushrooms to the chicken stock, bring to the boil, then simmer 15 minutes.
2. Add the ham slices and simmer 1-2 minutes. Taste for salt, then ladle into a soup tureen and serve immediately.

> *Points of interest*:
> Chinese soups should always be brought to the table in a handsome soup tureen then served individually into small bowls. The presentation of soup is always an occasion, a gesture of goodwill and good health.

Seafood and Spinach Soup

Ingredients:
6 cups clear chicken stock
1 teaspoon minced ginger
4 fresh prawns, cut into bite-sized pieces
4 fresh scallops, each cut into half
3 cups baby spinach leaves
2 teaspoons cornflour mixed with 2 tablespoons stock
1 egg, lightly beaten
Salt and pepper to taste

Cooking:
1. Heat chicken stock to just come to the boil. Add minced ginger, prawns and scallops.
2. When soup comes to the boil again, stir in the cornflour thickening, then add spinach leaves to soften. Just before serving, gently stir in the beaten egg, and add salt and pepper to taste.

Combination Soup

This soup is made from a little bit of this and a little bit of that, often from leftovers. The end result belies its humble beginnings and is a satisfying, tasty soup always enjoyed by the family. Translated in Chinese 'combination' means 'chop suey' hence, chop suey dishes are just that, a little bit of this and a little bit of that.

You will need:
1.5 litres (6 cups) chicken broth
60 g (2 oz) prawns or shrimps, deveined, washed, cut into bite-size pieces
120 g (4 oz) minced pork
250 g (8oz) Chinese wong buk cabbage or English spinach
4 Chinese dried mushrooms, soaked 30 minutes, stems removed and sliced into halves
¼ cup bamboo shoots, cut into julienne strips
15 g (½ oz) cellophane noodles, soaked 5 minutes and cut into 15 cm (6 inch) lengths
½ teaspoon salt, dash white pepper

Marinade for prawns:
2 teaspoons Chinese (Shaohsing) rice wine
1 teaspoon cornflour
1 teaspoon minced ginger

Marinade for minced pork:
½ teaspoon salt, pinch white pepper
1 teaspoon dry sherry
1 teaspoon cornflour
A little beaten egg

Preparation :
1. Marinate the prawns. Marinate minced pork and form into teaspoon size balls.
2. Wash Chinese cabbage or spinach and cut crosswise into 10 cm (4 inch) lengths.

Cooking :
1. Heat the chicken broth, add mushrooms, bamboo shoots and pork balls. Simmer for 10 minutes, the add pawns, noodles and cabbage with salt to simmer for another 5 minutes.
2. Ladle into a large soup tureen, arranging each ingredient in a separate section for an attractive presentation.

Chicken Wine Soup

You will need:
½ tender chicken
30 g (1 oz) smoked ham, cut into slices 5 mm (¼ inch) thick, 1 cm (2 inches) long by 2.5 cm (1 inch) wide
6 medium sized Chinese dried mushrooms, soaked 30 minutes, stalks removed
1.25 litres (5 cups) water
2 slices ginger
1½ teaspoons salt
1 tablespoon brandy

Cooking:
1. Wash chicken well and place in a large pyrex bowl with mushrooms, ginger, ham and water. Cover with lid or aluminium foil. Place bowl in a pot with enough water to come quarter way up and steam for 2 hours. A double boiler may be used instead. Add salt, brandy and serve in a large soup tureen.
2. The chicken is not carved before coming to the table, but will be tender enough for breaking up in the soup with chopsticks. This soup is really a meal in itself, the chicken being the main meat dish.

> ***Points of interest:***
> This is a special winter soup, rich and warming and full of mellow flavours. If a few extras like Chinese red dates and raw peanuts are added, then according to our ancient (and modern) beliefs, it has medicinal value. When taken by a new mother, it restores her spirits, chases away depression, at the same time restoring her body to prebirth fitness. New fathers would benefit too, I'm sure!

Velvet Chicken and Sweet Corn Soup

You will need:
1.5 litres (6 cups) chicken stock (made from whole chicken less the breasts)
2 chicken breasts, skinned
470 g (15 oz) can creamed sweet corn
2 eggs

Mix together:
1 teaspoon salt
4 tablespoons cold water

Thickening:
3 tablespoons cornflour mixed in a little cold chicken stock

Garnish:
3 tablespoons chopped spring onions or finely minced ham

Preparation:
1. Make the stock the day beforehand, skim and strain.
2. Slice, then mince the chicken with the chopper, add salted water a little at a time, beating in by hand, as in creaming butter and sugar. This makes 'velvet chicken'.
3. Beat the eggs lightly.

Cooking:
1. Add the velvet chicken a little at a time to the warm stock, bring gradually to the boil.
2. Add sweet corn, simmer 5 minutes, thicken with cornflour paste stirring until it comes to a gentle boil. Turn off the heat and gently stir in the lightly beaten eggs. Serve sprinkled with spring onions or ham.

> **Points of interest:**
> The soup can be prepared beforehand up to the stage of adding the eggs, and gently re-heated before serving.

Fresh Peas and Pork Ball Soup

Quite a different pea soup to the English split pea soup, I hope you like it as well, remember, fresh peas, not frozen!

You will need:
1.5 litres (6 cups) chicken or pork stock
1 cup fresh shelled peas
6 medium sized Chinese dried mushrooms, soaked 30 minutes
1/2 cup water chestnuts, sliced into halves horizontally
3 slices of ginger
2 eggs, lightly beaten
Salt to taste

Pork balls:
125 g (4 oz) minced pork or chicken
1/4 cup water chestnuts, finely chopped
1/4 cup spring onions, finely chopped
1/2 teaspoon salt
A little beaten egg, taken from the 2 eggs above
2 teaspoons cornflour

Preparation:
1. Mix all ingredients for pork balls in a bowl and shape into balls the size of a small walnut.

Cooking:
1. Add ginger, mushrooms, water chestnuts and peas to chicken stock and simmer for 10 minutes.
2. Add pork balls and simmer for a further 5 minutes. Add salt to taste.
3. Remove from heat and gently stir in eggs.

Chicken and Asparagus Soup

You will need:
1.5 litres (6 cups) chicken broth
60 g (2 oz) chicken meat
6 Chinese dried mushrooms
185 g (6 oz) tender fresh asparagus
2 eggs, lightly beaten
Salt to taste
A little light soy
A little Chinese (Shaohsing) rice wine
Cornflour

Preparation:
1. Soak the mushrooms for 30 minutes in warm water. Cut off the stems then slice each into 2 or 3 pieces.
2. Cut the chicken into pieces 5 cm by 2.5 cm (2 inch by 1 inch). Marinate lightly with a splash of light soy, dry sherry and cornflour. Place aside.
3. Break off the tough ends of asparagus stems, the tender part automatically snaps off from the tough ends. Roll cut into 5 cm (2 inch) lengths.

Cooking:
1. Add the mushrooms to simmer in the chicken broth for 10 minutes, then add the chicken slices and asparagus for a further 5 minutes, with lid off.
2. Season to taste, turn off heat and stir in the beaten eggs.

> ***Points of interest***:
> You already have the chicken broth from cooking white cut chicken in this menu. Always make the greatest use of ingredients in season. When asparagus is in season, cook it often and in as many different ways as you can think of.

Introduction to Seafood

"Out in the garden in the moonlight, our servant is scraping a golden carp with so much vigour that the scales fly in every direction, perhaps they go as high as heaven. Those beautiful stars up there might be the scales of our fish.'

'Before the Repast', author unknown

The Chinese prepare wonderful fish and seafood dishes. The first secret lies in freshness and that is why you will see so many Chinese at the fish markets. The second secret lies in the way it is cooked. The best fish is cooked whole, because that way it retains its juices better than when cut up. The most popular way to cook fish is by steaming and once again, the secret lies in its simplicity. Fresh ginger and spring onions are always used to eliminate 'fishy' odours and fish and seafoods are cooked until only 'just done'.

Top of the list in seafoods is fish, appropriately the Chinese character for fish 'Yui' means prosperity and abundance. Fish also symbolize regeneration and conjugal bliss as they often swim in pairs. Whole fish garnished with orange segments is often served at business dinners; the fish represents good luck and prosperity and the oranges symbolize gold!

How difficult is it to pick fresh fish in Australia when they are already dead? Be sure that the fish has bright, protruding eyes, that the gills are bright red and the flesh firm to touch. As soon as you can, wash and clean it thoroughly under cold running water, pat dry with a paper towel, sprinkle lightly with salt inside and out, and place in the refrigerator. We do not like to buy today's fish for tomorrow - the Chinese are very sensitive about the freshness of seafoods.

Fried Fish Rolls

You will need:
250 g (8 oz) thin fish fillets, flathead fillets are quite good, or you can slice up thicker fillets like rock ling or barramundi
1 teaspoon ginger juice (use garlic crusher)
1/2 teaspoon salt, dash white pepper
4 slices ham, shredded
Small amount of spinach which has been plunged into boiling water for one minute
Oil for deep frying

The batter:
1 cup self raising flour with a pinch of salt
1 egg
125 ml (1/2 cup) water

Cooking:
1. Cut fillets into pieces 10 cm by 4 cm wide (4 inches long by 1 1/2 inches) approximately.
2. Season with ginger juice, salt and pepper.
3. Lay a little ham and spinach on top of each fillet and roll up. Secure with a toothpick.
4. Coat lightly with batter and deep-fry until golden brown and crisp.

Sauteed Squid with Capsicums and Onions

Ingredients:
1/2 kg fresh squid
Capsicum
Onion

Light Batter:
1 cup SR flour
1/2 teaspoon baking powder
Cold water
A little clean peanut oil

Preparation:
1. Wash and score squid as directed.
2. Slice vegetables as directed.
3. Prepare spicy salt. Mix 1 tablespoon cooking salt, 1/4 teaspoon, 5 spice powder together and gently fry in a pre-heated dry wok or pan over low heat until salt changes colour and the mix is fragrant.

Cooking:
1. Heat oil ready for deep frying.
2. Dip each piece of squid into the batter wiping off excess and deep fry until lighly golden and crisp.
3. Heat wok, add a little peanut oil and quickly saute onions and capsicums until glazed and barely softened. add squid toss and tumble quickly, season with spicy salt and serve immediately.

Steamed Black Bean Fish

You will need:
1 whole fish, approximately 500 g (1 lb), bream, snapper, flounder, whiting, John Dory, trout, Murray perch, trevally
Sprinkle of salt, pepper, sesame oil and cornflour

The sauce:
1 tablespoon pickled black beans (dow si)
1 clove crushed garlic
1 tablespoon finely slivered ginger
1 tablespoon oil
1/4 teaspoon salt
1 tablespoon Chinese (Shaohsing) rice wine
1 tablespoon light soy
2 stalks spring onions, slivered
Extra 2 tablespoons oil

Preparation:
1. Wash and dry the fish thoroughly, then sprinkle with salt, pepper, sesame oil and cornflour and place on a plate ready for steaming.
2. Rinse black beans quickly in warm water, then place in a bowl and lightly crush with garlic. There is no need to crush the black beans to a paste. Add all ingredients except spring onions. Pour over the fish, adding spring onions on top.
3. Place the plate with fish on to a steaming rack over boiling water and steam over moderate heat for 15 minutes. The eye of the fish will protrude and turn white when cooked.
4. Heat the 2 tablespoons of oil in a small saucepan until smoking (watch over it!) Bring the fish to the saucepan and pour the smoking oil over the entire fish. Garnish with fresh spring onion slivers to serve.

Crispy Prawn Balls

These make very luxurious hors d'oeuvres and they can be served as a part of a Chinese dinner.

You will need:
375 g (12 oz) green prawns or shrimps
90 g (3 oz) pork fat
7 slices of white bread

'A':
1 teaspoon finely minced ginger
1 tablespoon finely chopped spring onion
1/2 teaspoon salt
1/4 teaspoon white pepper
1/2 tablespoon Chinese (Shaohsing) rice wine
1 egg white
2 tablespoons cornflour

Dip: mix together
1 tablespoon tomato sauce
2 teaspoons Worcestershire sauce

Garnish:
Crisp lettuce leaves
Oil for deep-frying

Preparation:
1. Smash shrimps or prawns heavily with the broad part of the chopper, then finely chop. Mince pork fat, mix together and chop again for another minute.
2. Prepare 'A' ingredients and mix through prawn mixture.
3. Remove the crusts from the toast and cut into very small cubes approximately 5 mm (1/4 inch) square.
4. Shape prawn mince mixture into balls about the size of a walnut. Roll in bread cubes.

Cooking:
1. Heat the oil in the wok to moderate heat and deep-fry until crisp and golden (about 2-3 minutes). Remove and serve on a bed of lettuce with dip.

Imperial Prawns – A Palace Dish

Ingredients:
375g king prawns – top quality, fresh!

Marinade:
A sprinkle of salt and pepper
A little peanut oil
2 tablespoons self raising flour
2 tablespoons potato flour

'A'
½ small red and ½ green capsicum, sliced
1 small onion, sliced
1 dried chilli pepper, seeds removed and chopped
1 large clove garlic, finely sliced
2 teaspoons finely sliced ginger

'B'
2 tablespoons sugar
2 tablespoons white vinegar
2 tablespoons light soy sauce
2 tablespoons Chinese (Shaohsing) rice wine

A little thickening made by mixing cornflour with a little water

Preparation:
1. Remove veins from prawns and wash well under cold running water. Pat dry with paper towels, and marinate while you prepare the other ingredients.
2. Combine the self raising flour and cornflour and lightly toss through the prawns. Add a little cold water to create a light batter over the prawns, and mix through quickly to combine.

Cooking:
1. Heat the wok, add oil and bring to a high heat. Reduce heat slightly and deep fry the prawns for approx. 3-4 minutes, gently stirring around with the chopsticks to separate and obtain an even cooking. During the last few seconds of cooking, add the onion and capsicums in the wok to blanch for about 5 seconds. Remove all ingredients with a strainer and place aside on a plate.
2. Drain off the oil, leaving a good film behind. Sizzle 'A' for a few seconds then add 'B'. Stir to combine, bring to the boil, then add a little thickening to obtain a light velvety consistency. Return the prawns and vegetables toss through quickly and serve.

Stir-Fried Prawns and Broccoli

You will need:
250 g (8 oz) green prawns
4 tablespoons oil
2 thin slices ginger
2 cups broccoli, cut into 6 cm (2 ½ inch) lengths
1 cup water chestnuts, sliced into halves horizontally
6 medium sized Chinese dried mushrooms (soaked 30 minutes and cut into halves) or 1 cup straw mushrooms

Marinade for prawns:
Dash salt and pepper
A little egg white
Dusting of cornflour

Seasoning:
2 teaspoons light soy sauce
1 tablespoon Chinese (Shaohsing) rice wine
1 teaspoon sugar
2 teaspoons sesame oil
½ teaspoon salt

Thickening:
2 teaspoons cornflour dissolved in 125 ml (½ cup) chicken stock or water

Preparation:
1. Cut half way through back of the prawns and remove the black thread. Wash well under cold running water, drain and pat dry thoroughly with a paper towel. Marinate with salt and pepper and egg white then dust with a little cornflour. Place on a plate with the 2 slices of ginger.
2. Bring a small pot of water to the boil, plunge broccoli for 1 minute. Rinse under cold water, drain well and place on a plate with water chestnuts and mushrooms.
3. Mix seasoning in a bowl. Mix thickening in a bowl.

Cooking:
1. Into a heated wok, add oil and 3 slices of ginger, swirling gently around sides of wok until it just begins to smoke. Add the prawns and stir-fry quickly over high heat for 2 minutes. The prawns will turn pink and become firmer.
2. Add mushrooms, water chestnuts and broccoli and continue to stir-fry over high heat a further 2 minutes. Add seasoning combining well for 30 seconds, then push ingredients to the sides of the wok and add thickening into centre of the pan stirring constantly until sauce thickens and becomes clear. Mix sauce through to coat and serve immediately.

Points of interest:
    It is essential to understand that the characteristics of stir-fried dishes are freshness, natural flavour and good texture. In order to achieve these results, time and heat are the two crucial elements.
    In Chinese cooking all green vegetables such as broccoli should be a brighter green after you cook them.

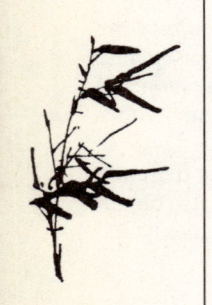

Satay Prawns

Satay dishes are not strictly Chinese, but belong to South-East Asian countries where there is a blending of many cuisines. The Chinese who live in these countries have taken the satay sauce and used it in their cuisine, thus making it 'Chinese' for those who live there. Overseas students from these areas living now in Australia have had quite an influence in introducing and popularizing Malaysian dishes alongside the more familiar Cantonese dishes from Hong Kong.

You will need:
500 g (1 lb) green prawns
1 medium sized brown onion
1 green capsicum
4 tablespoons peanut oil

Marinade for prawns:
1 tablespoon satay sauce
1 teaspoon curry powder
1/2 teaspoon chilli sauce or chilli oil
1 teaspoon light soy sauce
1 tablespoon Chinese (Shaohsing) rice wine
1 teaspoon minced ginger
1/2 teaspoon sugar
Dash salt and pepper
1/4 teaspoon five-spice powder
1 teaspoon cornflour

Garnish:
Crisp lettuce leaves
125 ml (1/2 cup) warmed brandy

Preparation:
1. Devein, wash and pat dry the prawns. When deveining, cut half through prawn - this opens it up so that it curls attractively when cooked. Add the prawns to the satay marinade and stand for 1 hour.
2. Cut the onion into half, then each half into four. Cut the capsicum into wedge shapes.

Cooking:
1. Heat the oil in the wok to moderate heat, stir-fry onions and capsicum until just softened (1-2 minutes). Be careful not to scorch them in oil that is too hot. Remove.
2. Turn up the heat. Add the prawns to the wok and stir-fry over maximum heat until they turn pink and become firm and bouncy (2-3 minutes). Return the onions and capsicum and a little water if necessary. Toss together then remove from wok.
3. Arrange the prawns on lettuce leaves on a serving plate. Warm up 125 ml (1/2 cup) brandy in a metal bowl, set it alight and place in the centre of the plate. Each prawn should be held over the brandy flame for a few seconds before eating.

Sliced Fish and Seasonal Vegetables

You will need:
315 g (10 oz) boneless, skinned fish fillets, rock ling, flathead, snapper, kingfish or any firm white fish is suitable
1/2 teaspoon salt
6 tablespoons peanut oil
3 thin slices ginger
1 stalk spring onion, chopped into 5 cm (2 inch) lengths

Marinade for fish:
1 egg white, lightly beaten
2 teaspoons Chinese (Shaohsing) rice wine
1/2 teaspoon salt, 1/4 teaspoon white pepper
2 teaspoons cornflour

Vegetables:
125 g (4 oz) snow peas (substitute asparagus or broccoli)
2 cups celery, diagonally sliced into 5 cm (2 inch) lengths
1 tablespoon cloud ear fungus (soaked 30 minutes, rinsed and drained)

Seasoning:
1 tablespoon light soy
2 teaspoons sesame oil
2 teaspoons Chinese (Shaohsing) rice wine
1/2 teaspoon sugar

Thickening:
1 1/2 teaspoons cornflour mixed in 65 ml (1/4 cup) chicken stock or water

Preparation:
1. Wash fillets under cold running water, pat dry with paper towel and cut into slices 2 cm wide by 5 cm (2 inches long).
2. Toss fish slices in marinade, then lightly coat with cornflour.
3. Bring some water to the boil in a saucepan and plunge the carrots, snow peas and celery for one minute. Rinse under cold water, drain well and place on a plate with the cloud ear fungus.

Cooking:
1. In a hot wok, add 6 tablespoons of oil, then ginger slices - swirl around sides of wok until just smoking. Reduce heat a little, deep-fry fish slices with spring onions for about 1 minute (until fish is white and firm) transfer to a heated plate. Drain off the oil, leaving 1 tablespoon of oil in the wok
2. In the remaining oil, add (1/2 teaspoon salt, stir for 30 seconds, then add the snow peas, celery, carrots and cloud ear fungus. Toss quickly to coat with oil for 1-2 minutes. Add seasonings, combine well for 30 seconds, then add thickening to the centre of the wok stirring until thickened and clear.
3. Return fish slices to wok and quickly combine with the vegetables. Serve hot.

Seafood in Claypot

Ingredients:
8 scallops
8 fresh (green) prawns, shells removed and de-veined
1 medium calamari
2 fillets flathead
4 fresh mussels in shells, cleaned thoroughly of sand and grit
4-5 good lettuce leaves, blanch quickly in boiling water then refreshen under cold water
1 cup peanut oil
1 knob fresh ginger, size of a small walnut, peeled and smashed with the flat of a heavy knife
3 spring onions, mainly white parts
1/4 teaspoon salt
1/4 teaspoons sugar
1/2 teaspoon sesame oil
1 1/2 cups chicken stock
2 teaspoons cornflour mixed in a little cold water for thickening
1 packet egg noodles (375 g) available at Asian stores
1/2 cup Chinese (Shaohsing) rice wine

Preparation:
1. Clean and score crisscross pattern on the inside section of the calamari. Cut into approximately 5 cm (2 inch) pieces.
2. Slice flathead fillets into thick slices.
3. Bring a pot of water to boil, add a little salt, and a few drops of cooking oil to the water, then blanch the seafood, excepting the mussels, over high heat. Remove with a slotted spoon even before the water returns to the boil. Drain and rinse gently under cold running water, them put aside.

Cooking:
1. Heat the oil in a pre-heated wok until moderately hot. Add the ginger and spring onions, then add all the seafood. Stir fry for about 2-3 minutes.
2. Add salt, sugar, sesame oil and the chicken stock. Immediately stir in the thickening until you have a velvety sauce that clings around the seafood pieces. Put aside while you cook the noodles.
3. Cook the noodles in a large pot of boiling water until 'al dente' if the noodles are fresh they need only to be soaked in hot water 3-4 minutes. Drain and rinse gently under cold water.
4. Arrange the blanched lettuce leaves at the bottom of the claypot, then place the noodles over the lettuce. Place the seafood over the noodles and pour enough of the liquid from the wok into the clay plot to a depth of about 2.5 cm (1 inch). Place on a moderately hot stove and cook until the steam bursts through the lid. The lid is then lifted off for every one to experience the first breath of its fragrance.

Grape Cluster Fish

Ingredients :
375-440 g (12-14 oz) thick central piece of white fish fillet preferably with skin on
1 teaspoon grated fresh ginger
1 tablespoon finely shopped spring onion
1 teaspoon salt
1 1/2 cups (185 g) cornflour
Oil for deep-frying
Grapevine leaves and stem for garnish

Sauce:
3 tablespoons chicken stock
3/4 cup dark grape juice
1 1/2 tablespoons red (Chin Kiang) vinegar
2 tablespoons light soy sauce
1 teaspoon sugar
1/2 teaspoon salt
1 tablespoon cornflour
1/2 teaspoon cooking oil

Preparation:
1. Place the piece of fish, skin side downwards, on a cutting board and cut a criss-cross pattern diagonally across it, cutting down to the skin but not through it. Place in a dish and scatter on the ginger, onion and salt. Leave for 15 minutes, then coat thickly with cornflour.

Cooking:
1. In a small wok or saucepan, boil the pre-mixed sauce ingredients for about 3 minutes, stirring constantly check the seasoning and keep warm.
2. Heat the oil in a large wok to smoking point, then reduce the heat slightly. Slide in the fish, skin side upwards, and deep-fry for about 5 minutes until golden and cooked through. As it cooks, the skin will curl up, giving the fish the appearance of a bunch of grapes.
3. Drain, place on a dish and arrange the vine leaves and stem at the top of the 'bunch of grapes'. Pour the sauce on and serve.

Crisp Fried Garfish

Victorian fish markets have a fairly constant supply of really fresh garfish all the year round. If you buy them straight from the fisherman's catch, the natural sweetness of this fish is superb. The price is usually reasonable, so garfish is economical and this simple way of preparing it is a firm family favourite.

You will need:
4 medium sized garfish or similar
Salt and pepper
Cornflour
Peanut oil
4 slices ginger
1 tablespoon light soy sauce
1 stalk spring onion, chopped

Preparation:
1. Wash and scale the fish under cold running water. Pat dry with paper towels.
2. Lay each fish, open side down on the chopping board and slap with the wide part of the chopper. (The main bone is then easily removed before or after cooking and the remaining tiny bones are eaten.) The fish is now somewhat flattened. Sprinkle with salt and pepper then dust with a little cornflour.

Cooking:
1. Cut off a section of fresh ginger and rub the base of your frying pan or wok with the exposed end, for 2-3 minutes while gently heating the pan. If you do this, the fish will not break when you turn it over.
2. Add enough oil to generously cover the bottom of the pan or wok, simmer the ginger slices in the oil until the oil just begins to smoke. Carefully slide in the garfish and fry over fairly hot oil until sides are crispy (about 3 minutes). Reduce heat, then turn the fish over. Increase heat, and fry for another 2 minutes.
3. Reduce heat to low, add 1 tablespoon soy sauce and chopped spring onions and simmer for 30 seconds. Remove to a heated plate and serve.

Prawn Balls and Snow Peas

These little soft hearted balls are deliciously attractive with pale pink hue against the jade green snow peas. If you are feeling in a poetic mood, you might like to call the dish 'Pearls and Jade'.

You will need:
500 g (1 lb) fresh prawns, deveined and washed
Oil for deep-frying

Prawn mince:
1 teaspoon finely minced ginger
1/2 cup water chestnuts, finely chopped
1 teaspoon salt, dash white pepper
1 teaspoon Chinese (Shaohsing) rice wine
1/2 egg white, lightly beaten with 2 teaspoons cornflour

Simmering sauce:
250 ml (1 cup) chicken stock
1 teaspoon oyster sauce

Thickening for sauce:
1 tablespoon cornflour in 1 tablespoon water

The snow peas:
500 g (1 lb) snow peas, topped, tailed and washed
1/2 teaspoon salt
1 teaspoon sugar
125 ml (1/2 cup) water

Cooking:
1. Chop the prawns to a mince and add all other ingredients.
2. Shape into balls (walnut size) and deep-fry until golden and crisp (3-4 minutes).
3. Simmer in simmering sauce 5 minutes.
4. Meanwhile, stir-fry snow peas in a saucepan with salt, toss until glazed, add sugar, then water, cover and cook for 1-2 minutes. Serve on to a heated plate, arrange prawn balls on top.
5. Stir in cornflour thickening into sauce until it becomes clear and thickens and spoon over prawn balls.

Note: Sauce should be clear and of a good holding consistency and should not run off the prawn balls on to the peas. The peas should be kept clean and crisp

Stuffed King Prawns

You will need:
6 shelled fresh king prawns deveined, washed and patted dry.
1 1/2 cups breadcrumbs
Oil for deep-frying

The stuffing:
250 g (8 oz) extra prawns or crab meat, chopped to a mince (these do not have to be king prawns; the smaller variety is quite adequate and much cheaper)
60 g (2 oz) pork mince
1 teaspoon salt, dash pepper
1/2 egg beaten
2 teaspoons cornflour

The batter:
1 cup self raising flour with a pinch of salt
Enough cold water to mix to a 'holding' consistency

Plum and hoi sin sauce dip: Mix together
1 teaspoon hoi sin sauce
1 teaspoon plum sauce
1/4 teaspoon vinegar
1/2 teaspoon dark soy sauce

Preparation:
1. Mix all stuffing ingredients in a bowl and beat together until quite firm (similar method to creaming butter and sugar). Refrigerator to firm up for an hour.
2. Cut a small slit on the underside of each prawn, this prevents the prawn from curling. Spread the stuffing along the open belly of the prawns pressing the stuffing mixture firmly with the fingers. Dip each prawn into the batter, then coat heavily with the breadcrumbs on both sides. Continue until all prawns are coated.

Cooking:
Heat oil for deep-frying to moderate, add prawns singly and deep-fry until crisp and golden, about 3 minutes. Serve on heated plate with plum and hoi sin sauce dip.

> ***Points of interest:***
> The prawns can be prepared (up to the batter stage) a day earlier and kept in the refrigerator until ready for deep-frying.

Prawn Stuffed Mushrooms

'A well prepared mushroom should literally squirt its juices against the cheeks of the mouth until it fills the whole palate with voluptuous delight!

Lin Yutang

You will need:
12 thick round dried Chinese mushrooms (top grade)

Simmering sauce:
2 tablespoons oil
250 ml (1 cup) chicken stock
1 tablespoon dark soy sauce
1 teaspoon sugar
1 teaspoon salt
1 clove star anise
1 tablespoon Chinese (Shaohsing) rice wine

Thickening:
1 tablespoon cornflour dissolved in 1 tablespoon water

The prawn stuffing: Place all ingredients into a bowl and mix to a mince mixture
250 g (8 oz) fresh prawns, chopped to a rough mince
125 g (4 oz) pork mince (fatty)
1 teaspoon ginger juice (use garlic crusher)
1 1/2 teaspoons salt; 1/4 teaspoon pepper
1 teaspoon Chinese (Shaohsing) rice wine
2 teaspoons cornflour
1/2 egg white

Extra:
1 head of lettuce
1 teaspoon salt
1 teaspoon sugar
2 cloves finely minced garlic
3 tablespoons oil

Preparation:
1. Soak mushrooms for 30 minutes in warm water, rinse well, then re-soak a further 30 minutes. Squeeze out excess water, remove and discard stalks.
2. In a saucepan saute mushrooms gently in 2 tablespoons oil 2-3 minutes. Add simmering sauce and cook gently 15 minutes. Remove mushrooms and put aside. Reserve sauce.
3. Stuff each mushroom with a generous amount of the prawn mixture, shaping the top into a smooth mound.
4. Separate and wash each lettuce leaf under cold running water. Break off any tough stems.

Cooking :
1. Place stuffed mushrooms on an oiled plate and steam 10 minutes.
2. When stuffed mushrooms are almost ready, add 3 tablespoons oil to a saucepan or the wok, add 1 teaspoon salt and when just smoking, stir-fry garlic, salt, and lettuce leaves for 1-2 minutes. You will need to have a medium-to-large size saucepan as the lettuce takes a fair amount of room until it begins to soften and cook down. When that happens, add sugar, cover with lid and cook 30 seconds longer. Remove to a heated serving plate.
3. Bring simmering sauce back to boiling, stir in cornflour thickening to a holding consistency, then add rice wine.
4. Remove stuffed mushrooms from the steamer, arrange on top of the braised lettuce (prawn side up). Spoon the sauce over the mushrooms.

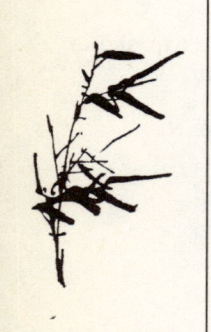

Simplicity Ginger Fish

You will need:

1 whole fish: coral trout, Murray perch, bream, snapper or similar
3 tablespoons fresh ginger, shredded
3 tablespoons light soy sauce
4 tablespoons peanut oil
1/2 teaspoon sugar
Spring onions, shredded

Marinade for fish:
Salt, pepper
2 teaspoons sesame oil
3 teaspoons cornflour

Preparation:
1. Sprinkle the fish with salt and pepper, sesame oil and cornflour and place on to a plate ready for steaming.
2. Arrange ginger slices and 1 tablespoon of the spring onions over the fish.

Cooking:
1. Place the plate with the fish on to a steaming rack or into a Chinese steaming basket and place in the wok over boiling water to steam for 15 to 20 minutes.
2. Remove from the steamer, sprinkle soy and remaining spring onions over the fish. Heat the oil in a small saucepan until just beginning to smoke and immediately pour over the fish. Garnish with fresh spring onions and serve immediately.

> **Points of interest:**
> The searing of very hot oil firms up the skin and texture of the fish and heightens the flavour of the ginger and spring onions.

Red Simmered Fish

Ingredients:
1 bream or similar fish (600-700 g)
Pepper
A little cornflour
3 slices ginger
4 tablespoons oil
Spring onions and red capsicum, shredded finely for garnish

Sauce:
1 teaspoon ground bean paste (available Asian stores)
1 tablespoon sweet chilli sauce (available Asian stores)
1 tablespoon light soy sauce
2 tablespoons Chinese (Shaohsing) rice wine
1 1/2 teaspoons sugar
1 teaspoon sesame oil
3 tablespoons red (Chin Kiang) vinegar
2 cloves garlic, peeled and lightly bruised
1 bird's eye chilli pepper, chopped
4 tablespoons chicken stock

Preparation:
Dust fish with a little pepper and cornflour
Make up sauce in a bowl

Cooking:
1. Heat the wok, add oil and ginger slices, swirling oil gently around the side of the wok. When the oil begins to smoke carefully slide in the fish and fry over moderate heat for 5 minutes each side.
2. Reduce heat to low, then add sauce and simmer a further 5 minutes with the lid on. Serve immediately.

Simplicity Ginger Fish - page 63

Red Simmered Fish -
page 64

Crisp Skin Chicken -
page 71

Braised Duckling with
Baby Bok Choy - page 76

Poultry

> 'I would rather eat 4 oz of the flying species than 4 lb of animals on land.'
> *Ancient Chinese Proverb*

Poultry is an important part of the Chinese diet, the meat is so versatile it can be cooked whole, or in pieces that are steamed, simmered, deep-fried and roasted. Besides that, it is often dried and salted and used as flavouring or as tasty tidbits at a meal. Chicken is used more often than duck in the everyday Chinese diet but duck comes close in popularity and enjoys high status at dinner parties.

When buying your chicken choose a plump bird that has smooth, moist skin. If the skin is yellowish, then it will be fatty and inclined to be a little on the elderly side; if the skin is satiny white, then the meat will be very tender. Nowadays, you can purchase chicken breasts, drumsticks and wings, instead of the whole chicken and in some stores, you can buy packs of chicken pieces for making stock. These are a little more expensive, but the convenience is often worthwhile as boning a chicken is not everybody's idea of fun.

Choosing a tender duck is not always as easy as choosing a young chicken. The Chinese pinch the windpipe and if it is elastic and supple to the touch then it is young, but I rather suspect our non-Chinese shopkeepers would not be too happy with customers who go around pinching ducks' necks. However, a plump bird with a moist not too yellow skin is a fair measure.

Never discard any unused portions like bones, giblets or necks of poultry, they can be frozen and used for making chicken stock.

Drunken Chicken

You will need:
1 size 12 chicken   1 cup Chinese (Shaohsing) rice wine
1½ teaspoons salt   1 extra tablespoon Chinese (Shaohsing) rice wine
3 teaspoons sugar

Preparation:
1. Place the chicken in a deep dish, gently rub salt and sugar on the outside and inside cavity of the chicken. Allow to marinate for approximately one hour.
2. Pour wine over the entire chicken (inside as well), marinate for a further 7 hours. Turn the chicken several times.

Cooking:
1. Place the chicken into the wok to steam. The chicken should be standing in wine and the dish can sit suspended on a rack over boiling water (a small cake rack would be suitable). Steam for 15 minutes, before turning the chicken to steam another 15 minutes. Remove from the wok, allow to cool, chop the chicken and arrange on a serving platter.
2. Use a coffee filter to strain the sauce obtained from the steaming, add the extra tablespoon of wine, and pour over the chicken just before serving. Serves 10 as an entree.

> ***Points of interest:***
> To chop it in the Chinese manner, use a cleaver to halve the bird along the breastbone. Cut wings and drumsticks away from the breast, remove bones, clip each joint and each breast into three.

Black Satin Chicken

The flavour and texture of this chicken dish is rather different from the usual chicken recipes. Do not attempt to chop the chicken while still hot, the flavour is at its best when eaten at room temperature. Avoid over cooking, Chinese chicken should be slightly 'pink' at the inner drumsticks and thigh joint and the juices should run when the thigh is separated from the body.

You will need:
1 roasting chicken, approximately 1.3 kg (2½ lb)
Knob of ginger, size of small walnut
1 stalk spring onion
3 extra spring onions for garnish

Marinade: Mix together
1 tablespoon Chinese (Shaohsing) rice wine
1 teaspoon salt
½ teaspoon pepper

Sauce:
250 ml (1 cup) dark soy sauce
2 tablespoons light soy sauce
250 ml (1 cup) water
½ cup soft brown sugar
2 teaspoons sesame oil
1 clove star anise
2 medium sized Chinese dried mushrooms (soaked 30 minutes)

Preparation:
1. Rub the marinade gently inside and outside of the chicken and let it stand for 30 minutes. Place the spring onion and ginger inside the chicken.
2. Combine the sauce ingredients together into a saucepan large enough to hold the chicken.

> *Points of interest:*
> The sauce can be kept for several months in the refrigerator. It will 'jell' when cold. Remember to boil it up once a week and it will be good for many black satin chickens.

Cooking :
1. Gently simmer the sauce in a saucepan until boiling, then place the chicken into the pot. After the sauce comes back to the boil, turn down to a low simmer. Spoon the sauce over the chicken and turn over on to the other side after the first 10 minutes. Turn again after another 10 minutes, spooning the sauce occasionally to colour the skin evenly. Be careful that the heat is not too high, as this could cause the skin to break.
2. Remove the chicken when cooked, 50 minutes should be enough, but it is cooked when the flesh on the drumstick has shrunk back from the bone. Cook the chicken to room temperature, then chop into Chinese chopstick sizes. Arrange on an oval plate, spoon over 2 tablespoons of the heated sauce and garnish with 3 spring onion brushes and the mushrooms.

Spring Onion Brushes

Cut off the roots of the spring onion stalks, and cut off sections about 7.5 cm (3 inches) up. Insert a sewing needle completely through the stalk about 2.5 cm (1 inch) from the bottom and tear up to the other end to form shreds. Make approximately 6 insertions and repeat. Put into a bowl of water with ice cubes and they will curl up in about 30 minutes.

Spicy Chicken Drumsticks or Wings
(Serve hot or cold)

I find these very good to serve at casual parties where people stand around with a drink in one hand and something to eat in the other. With their hot, spicy flavour they make a change from the usual cold meats. The coating sauce, whilst delicious, can be a little messy so a little wrapping of silver foil around the bone keeps your fingers clean and adds a glamour touch at the same time.

You will need:
10 chicken drumsticks or
10 chicken wings, cut into half, tips discarded (keep for soup)
125 ml (1/2 cup) light soy
1 tablespoon Chinese (Shaohsing) rice wine
2 tablespoons honey
1 chopped hot chilli pepper or 1 teaspoon chilli sauce
2 tablespoons water
1 clove garlic (chopped)
Pinch five spice powder

Preparation :
1. Marinate drumsticks or wings for 1 hour.

Cooking :
1. Bake in pre-heated oven 180°C (375°F) for 45 minutes.

Hoi Sin Chicken

You will need:
500 g (1 lb) chicken fillets (Cut into pieces about 5 cm by 2.5 cm (2 inches by 1 inch).
1 clove crushed garlic
2 tablespoons hoi sin sauce

Marinade:
½ egg white
¼ teaspoon salt
1 tablespoon cornflour

Seasoning: Mix in a bowl
½ tablespoon dark soy sauce
1 tablespoon Chinese (Shaohsing) rice wine
2 teaspoons sugar
1 teaspoon sesame oil

Preparation :
1. Marinate chicken for 10 minutes.

Cooking :
1. Heat the wok and when just smoking, add the chicken pieces and fry over moderate heat for 1 minute. Remove. Drain off oil, leaving 1 tablespoon behind.
2. Stir in crushed garlic and hoi sin sauce for 10 seconds, then return chicken and seasonings. Combine quickly for sauce to coat and serve garnished with spring onion curls (see Black Satin Chicken recipe) or sprigs of coriander (Chinese parsley).

Roast Cantonese Chicken

You will need:
1 plump roasting chicken, approximately 1.5 kg (3 lb)

'A':
1 clove garlic
2 slices ginger
1 spring onion
1 tablespoon sugar
1 teaspoon salt
2 teaspoons Chinese (Shaohsing) rice wine
1 tablespoon light soy sauce

'B':
2 tablespoons white vinegar
1 tablespoon light soy sauce
1 teaspoon sugar
1 tablespoon water

> ***Points of interest***:
> Do not rub the soy sauce on the skin of the chicken with the fingers as this will darken areas and cause ugly blotches.
> Do not over-cook. The skin should be golden brown, not dark brown. If the meat has been allowed to become dry, then 'the chicken has died in vain'.
> The flavour of whole cooked chicken is often more appreciated when eaten at room temperature.

Preparation :
1. With a length of string, tie a knot very tightly around the neck of the chicken.
2. Place garlic, ginger, spring onion, sugar and salt inside the chicken's cavity.
3. Close up opening in chicken (I actually use needle and thread and sew it up with a blanket stitch), you could use some fine skewers. Add light soy sauce and wine just before finishing your needlework.
4. Place the chicken in a strainer over the sink and thoroughly scald it by pouring a large kettle of boiling water over the entire bird. The chicken will plump and firm out and the skin will become satin smooth and tight, a fantastic facial treatment!
5. Put 'B' in a small saucepan and bring to the boil. Pour over the chicken. Repeat until the skin of the chicken has been entirely covered by the sauce. Don't worry that the skin has not darkened yet, it will once it starts cooking in the oven.

Cooking :
1. Place on a rack in the middle of the oven 235°C (450°F) over a pan that is on the lowest rung holding about 5 mm (1/4 inch) of water. When the colour begins to turn a light golden (approximately 10 minutes) turn oven down to 175°C (350°F) for approximately 30 minutes, then 130°C (280°F) for 15 minutes. The complete cooking time for the chicken should be approximately 55 minutes.
2. Allow to cool down a little, then chop up Chinese style. Serve on oval plate, garnished with spring onion curls.

White Cut Chicken with Ginger and Spring Onion Dip

This is a classic Chinese dish, beloved by all and is equally popular at lavish banquets or at the family meal. Its appeal lies in its simplicity, but simplicity can so easily and often be spoilt. Use fresh, not frozen chicken, as smooth silky texture of skin and moist juice meat is the aim of this dish. The Chinese 'seep' rather than boil chicken for fear of over-cooking. The cold water treatment after cooking 'firms' up the skin.

You will need:
1 roasting chicken, approximately 1.5 kg (3 lb)
A little extra salt
1 teaspoon salt
Knob ginger, size of small walnut
1 stalk spring onion
Water to cover chicken
1 tablespoon sesame oil

Dip: Place in a small saucer
1 teaspoon salt
2 teaspoons minced ginger
1/2 cup finely chopped spring onions
4 tablespoons peanut oil

Preparation:
1. Wash the chicken well and pat dry with a paper towel inside and out. Gently rub some salt over the skin and let stand 30 minutes. This helps to prevent the skin from breaking.

Cooking:
1. Place the bird into a pot with enough cold water to cover, add 1 teaspoon salt, spring onion, ginger and bring to the boil. Cook the chicken on boiling for 5 minutes, then turn over to other side to cook for another 5 minutes. Turn off the heat and let stand 30 minutes. Remove from pot, gently run under cold water, then apply sesame oil over the skin.
2. Chop into 'chopstick' size pieces and arrange Chinese style on oval plate. Garnish with spring onion brushes or curls (see recipe for black satin chicken) and serve with the ginger and spring onion dip.

The dip:
Heat the 4 tablespoons of oil until just hot and pour over the salt, minced ginger and spring onions. Serve the dip in a small dish beside the chicken.

Crisp Skin Chicken

This is rightly a restaurant dish rather than a home dish, but I have so many requesting it that I now include it in my classes. It involves the complete immersion of a whole chicken in very hot oil. Restaurants have larger woks than the woks generally used at home and so the deep-frying of whole poultry does not present a problem. Apart from that I feel the procedure requires a certain degree of confidence for a wok full of very hot oil can be dangerous if you are an inexperienced cook. However, even after stressing this factor, my students have been happily preparing crisp skin chicken without any undue stress. I do ask you to be careful, do not have too much oil in the wok so that it might overflow once you lower the chicken into it and do keep small children safely away from the kitchen when you are deep-frying. It is not strictly correct, but you might prefer to fry the chicken in two halves rather than as a whole, but please don't ask a Chinese friend to dinner and pass the dish off as traditional crisp skin chicken!

When a chicken is deep-fried whole, the juices are kept better and the meat remains white, rather than browned from the oil. It is also the classic recipe for lemon chicken, the juice of fresh lemons being squeezed over the chopped crispy pieces at the table. Over recent years there have been a number of 'new' lemon chicken recipes, some good, some bad.

Ingredients:
1 roasting chicken - size 12 (for 4)

Glazing for skin:
1 cup water
1 cup white vinegar
1 tablespoon malt sugar - available Chinese stores
2 tablespoons Chinese (Shaohsing) rice wine
Oil for deep frying the chicken

Spicy salt: Mix together
3 teaspoons salt
1/2 teaspoon 5 spice powder

Garnish:
1/2 fresh lemon
Prawn crackers
Parsley

Preparation:
1. Wash and pat dry the chicken. Place half of the spicy salt into the cavity and rub well into the area. Gently rub remaining spicy salt over the entire skin and allow to stand 15 minutes. Place chicken under gently running cold water to remove excess salt and pat dry.
2. Combine the glazing ingredients in a small saucepan and heat gently until the malt sugar is dissolved, then rub the malt mixture over the entire skin of the chicken gently and evenly. Hang the chicken up to dry for a minimum of 2 hours.

Cooking:
1. Heat oil for deep frying the chicken until oil is just beginning to smoke (a narrow deep pot it ideal).
2. Carefully lower the chicken into the oil, maintaining a moderate heat while you ladle the hot oil over the skin. Once the skin is colouring a little, lower the heat, continuing to ladle the oil over the chicken and turning the chicken three or four times. Continue deep frying and ladling the oil for 15 minutes.
3. Remove the chicken from the oil carefully, draining it well. Raise the heat of the oil to just smoking again and return the chicken to the oil, ladling again until the skin is golden brown and crisp. Stand 15 minutes then chop into serving portions. Serve with fresh lemon and garnish with prawn crackers and parsley.

> *Points of interest:*
> This recipe is recommended for experienced cooks, because of the concentration needed to control the hot oil.

Chicken & Mushrooms in Plum Sauce

(A Rich Slow-Cooked Chinese Stew)

You will need:
750 g chicken pieces (with or without bones)
8 medium size Chinese black mushrooms (soak 30 minutes in warm water and remove stems)
8 medium size fresh mushrooms
Small knob fresh ginger, peeled and 'bruised'
2 stalks spring onions, cut into 5 cm sections

Marinade for chicken: Mix together and add to chicken
Salt and pepper
Few drops sesame oil
Splash Chinese (Shaohsing) rice wine
1 tablespoon cornflour

Braising sauce: mix together in a bowl
2 tablespoons Oyster sauce
2 teaspoons dark soy sauce
1/2 cup plum sauce
1 teaspoon sugar
1 cup chicken stock (or soaking water from mushrooms)

Final seasoning:
1 teaspoon sesame oil
1 teaspoon Chinese (Shaohsing) rice wine
1 tablespoon cornflour blended into 2 tablespoons water

Preparation:
1. Cut chicken into neat serving portions and marinate. Slice mushrooms and assemble sauce ready for use.

Cooking:
1. Heat wok, add a little cooking oil and brown chicken pieces. Remove to a plate.
2. Sauté ginger and spring onions briefly to release juices, add Chinese mushrooms, then return chicken to the wok. Stir-fry over high heat 1-2 minutes then add braising sauce. Combine well
3. Transfer all ingredients to a casserole dish. Simmer on top of the stove over low to moderate heat for 30 minutes, then add the fresh mushrooms to cook for 5 minutes before adding the final seasoning, stirring gently until sauce is velvety and bubbling (or cook in oven 180°C for 45 minutes).
4. Serve garnished with freshly sliced spring onions, and serve with Chinese stir-fried greens and noodles pasta or rice.

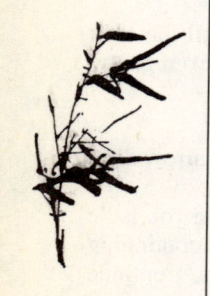

Lemon Chicken

You will need:
500 g (1 lb) chicken meat, breast of chicken mainly
Oil for deep-frying

Marinade for chicken:
Salt, dash white pepper
1/2 tablespoon Chinese (Shaohsing) rice wine
1/2 tablespoon light soy sauce
1 tablespoon water
1 egg yolk, lightly beaten
6 tablespoons cornflour } sifted together
3 tablespoons plain flour } on a plate

Sauce:
125 ml (1/2 cup) lemon juice
4 tablespoons sugar
3 teaspoons cornflour dissolved in a little lemon juice

Garnish:
6 lemon slices, parsley

Preparation:
1. Slice the chicken meat into pieces approximately 5 cm by 2.5 cm (2 inches long by 1 inch wide.)
2. Marinate for 15 minutes, then roll in mixed flours. Shake off excess flour.

Cooking:
1. Heat the oil for deep-frying to moderately hot and deep-fry chicken pieces for 2 minutes, dropping them one at a time into the oil. Drain on absorbent paper. This first frying can be done earlier in the day.
2. Heat the oil to smoking for the second deep-fry. Add all the chicken pieces into the hot oil at once and deep-fry over high heat for two more minutes. Remove and drain. Arrange on a heated serving plate.
3. In the time between the two fryings, make up the lemon sauce: Simmer together lemon juice sugar for 3 minutes, then stir in cornflour mixed with a little extra lemon juice until sauce becomes clear and thickens.

Just before serving, pour the lemon sauce over the chicken, garnish with fresh lemon slices and parsley.

> ***Points of interest:***
> The heat of the oil is not lessened too much when you drop the meat pieces in one at a time. It does not matter during the second frying process, as the meat juices have been retained by the first frying.

Cantonese Roast Duckling

These are the glowing chestnut-coloured ducks you see hanging suspended in the glassed partitions at the front of restaurants in the East. Chinese are very partial to roast duckling and often like to include this dish on special occasions. It is not necessary to serve roast duck piping hot, it is actually preferred at room temperature. The skin should be crisp, covering a succulent layer of fat and the meat tender and fragrant.

You will need:
1.5 kg (3 lb) young duckling

Marinade 'A': Mix together
1 tablespoon honey
Pinch red food colouring

Mixture 'B':
2 tablespoons bean sauce (min si jeung)
2 cloves peeled garlic, lightly slapped with the chopper
1 knob ginger, size of small walnut, bruised with the back of chopper
2 stalks spring onions
1 tablespoon Chinese (Shaohsing) rice wine
1 teaspoon sugar
1 teaspoon salt
2 tablespoons light soy sauce

Preparation:
1. Pour a kettle full of boiling water inside and over the outside of the duckling.
2. Gently rub 'A' mixture to coat the skin of the duck and hang it up in a draughty place (beside an open window) for 6 hours or overnight. Place a dish under the duck to catch the drips.
3. Put all the ingredients from mixture 'B' inside the duck and seal up the opening. You can either close the opening stitching with a needle and thread or fasten with some fine skewers.
4. Place the duck on a wire rack (a cake rack will do) and place the rack in the centre of a pre-heated oven 180°C (355°F). Place a tray containing a very small amount of water on the lowest shelf of the oven. Roast for 50 minutes, turning the duck once, then turn up the oven to 210°C (400°F) for the remaining 10 minutes. Remove and cool, then remove thread or skewers and pour off the juices into a small saucepan to heat up.
5. Chop up the duckling Chinese style. Spoon the hot sauce over and serve garnished with Chinese mixed pickles and spring onion brushes (see Black Satin Chicken recipe).

Lychee Mandarin Duckling

This is a good dish for entertaining as the preparation of the duck and the sauce can be done the day beforehand. Cooking time is very short.

You will need:
1 duck 1.5 - 2 kg (3-4 lb)
2 cloves anise
1 small knob ginger
1½ teaspoons salt
½ teaspoon five-spice powder (mix together)
3 egg yolks, lightly beaten
Oil for deep-frying
4 tablespoons plain flour   } mix together
4 tablespoons cornflour

Sauce:
½ orange, sliced in rings
250 ml (1 cup) duck stock
2 tablespoons vinegar
3 tablespoons sugar
1 tablespoon tomato sauce

Thickening for sauce:
½ teaspoons cornflour dissolved in a little lychee juice

Garnish:
½ can lychees
1 can mandarins

Preparation:
1. Simmer duck with anise and ginger in enough water to cover for 1½ hours or until soft. Remove and debone. Chop the duck into halves, and rub with salt and five-spice mixture. Stand 15 minutes.
2. Dust with half the amount of flour, then apply beaten egg yolks. Apply the remaining flour and lightly press on top.
3. Simmer sauce ingredients 5 minutes, stir in thickening.

Cooking:
1. Deep-fry duck halves one at a time in moderately hot oil until crisp and golden, about 3 minutes on each side. Remove, drain and chop straight across each half into slices about 4 cm (1½ inches) wide. Arrange on a heated serving plate, pour over hot sauce and garnish with lychees and mandarins.

Braised Duckling with Baby Bok Choy

You will need:
1 duck 1.5-2 kg (about 3½ lbs)
3 tablespoons dark soy sauce
1.5 litres (6 cups) oil, for deep-frying

Simmering sauce:
1.7 litres (7 cups) water
1 stalk spring onion, cut into 7.5 cm (3 inch) lengths
3 slices ginger
2 cloves star anise
½ cup soft brown sugar
1 teaspoon salt
2 tablespoons dry sherry or Chinese (Shaohsing) rice wine
2 tablespoons dark soy sauce
4 Chinese dried mushrooms (soaked 30 minutes & rinsed)

Preparation:
1. Wash and dry the duck thoroughly. Gently rub 3 tablespoons of dark soy over the skin. Allow to dry, either hang up or put on a wire cake cooler.

Cooking:
1. Deep-fry the duck in moderately hot oil until golden brown. Remove, drain off the oil. It is not practical for the home cook to use quantities of oil to completely cover the duck, so you could carefully turn it to brown evenly and constantly ladle hot oil over the exposed areas.
2. Heat all the sauce ingredients in a large saucepan for 2-3 minutes and place the duck in the pot, breast side down. Cover and bring to the boil quickly then reduce heat to gently cook for 2½ hours. You should turn the duckling at least twice in that time.
3. Cool a little before removing the duck from the pot. Slice and arrange on serving plate garnish with baby bok choy.
4. Baby bok choy. Cut each cabbage into quarters, trim off green leaves and wash well. Drop the cabbage stalks into a pot of boiling salted water for 1 minute. Remove, then sauté lightly in a little hot oil. Arrange around the duck, tucking the green ends under each stalk.

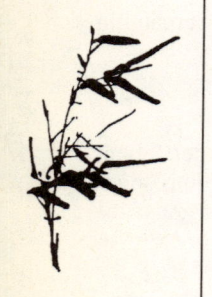

Pine Leaves Tea Smoked Duck

Ingredients:
1 whole Peking duck approx size 16

Marinade:
2 tablespoons salt
Good pinch roasted Sichuan peppercorn
3 cloves star anise
2 pieces fresh ginger, peeled, sliced and smashed
2 stalks spring onion
1 tablespoon Chinese (Shaohsing) rice wine
1 tablespoon peanut or vegetable oil

For frying:
1 tablespoon dark soy sauce

Preparation:
1. Rub marinade ingredients well into the cavity and the outside skin of the duck. Place star anise and some ginger and spring onion inside the duck. Marinate overnight. Rub soy over it and deep-fry till skin turns a rich dark brown.
2. Place duck on a steaming rack (cake rack will do), over boiling water and steam for about an hour.

The smoking: Mix together
Good handful of fresh pine needles
Small handful of cooked rice
2 tablespoons jasmine tea
2 tablespoons sugar

Preparation:
1. Place smoking ingredients into wok and heat until smoking.
2. Arrange cake rack in wok and place duck on the rack. When the smoke turns from white to yellow, switch off the flame. Cover with lid and smoke for another 2 minutes.

The deep-frying:
1. When the duck is cooked a little, deep-fry in just moderately hot oil for 5-7 minutes.
2. When the skin is golden brown remove.
3. Chop into sections Chinese style, or debone and slice.

Meats

'The chicken, the pig, the fish, the duck -
these are the four heroes of the table.'

Yuen Mai

Pork

Pork 'marries' well with other ingredients and unlike lamb does not posses a strong smell of its own. Unlike beef, pork has a smooth texture that respond well to any treatment from boiling to roasting and frying. The Chinese coo believes he should be the master who dictates the taste and texture of a dish an pork suits his purposes admirably.

Another reason for the popularity of pork is because pigs take up little spac in a land where 80 per cent of the people are farmers and every available inc of ground is used for the growing of rice crops and other vegetation. Pigs ar a part of a Chinese village household, take up little room and agreeably eat u scraps, so they virtually earn their own keep.

For very good reason then the Chinese character for 'home' is written up a a combination of a roof over a pig. The possession of a pig in a home is a toke of prosperity.

Beef

On the other hand, oxen are traditionally man's best friend, as they ar faithful and valuable helpers to a farmer. Their great strength and patience i pulling the plough is so appreciated, that there is an old Chinese saying that 'i times of trouble, it is better to sell one's wife than one's cow.' Thus to enjo eating beef inflicts feelings of guilt. From a more practical point of view, ther is once again the factor of space for grazing cattle. Generally speaking, littl beef is eaten today even by the wealthy who can afford it. The Chinese prefe white meat to red. Nevertheless, there are some excellent Chinese beef dishe and the popular and gourmet dishes featured by our restaurants reflect this.

Lamb

Lamb is eaten in northern China, but the southerners dislike its stron odour, considering it unsuitable to 'marry' with other ingredients.

A curious fact, though, is that roast lamb, English style, is well liked b Chinese who have settled in Western countries and is one of the first Englis dinners they learn to cook.

Sweet and Sour Pork

This is one of the most popular of all dishes to come out of the kitchen of Chinese restaurants in the West. The combination of sweet and sour in a sauce is an intriguing blend of flavours, but the dish can be destroyed by lack of understanding of how this sauce should be used. It is a glamorous dish with clear, sparkling colours, a tantalizing smell, crisp texture and interesting flavour. It certainly meets the requirements that 'every well prepared dish should please the four senses of man, sight, smell, feel and taste'.

You will need:
500 g (1lb) pork meat
Oil for deep frying

'A' - the pork
2 tablespoons light soy
1 tablespoon Chinese (Shaohsing) rice wine
3 tablespoons cornflour ⎫
3 tablespoons plain flour ⎭ mix together
3 egg yolks (lightly beaten)

'B' - the vegetables
1 medium red capsicum
1 medium green capsicum
1 medium sized white onion
1 small-medium sized carrot
1 cup pineapple pieces (canned or fresh)
1/2 cup Chinese mixed pickles

'C' - the sauce
4 tablespoons vinegar
4 tablespoons sugar
1 tablespoon light soy
1 tablespoon dry sherry
3 tablespoons tomato sauce
1 tablespoon juice from Chinese mixed pickles

Thickening:
2 rounded teaspoons cornflour dissolved in 1 tablespoon pineapple juice

Preparation:
1. Wedge cut vegetables. Plunge carrot wedges in boiling water for 2 minutes. Assemble together on one plate.
2. Cut the pork into 2.5 cm (1 inch) pieces, marinate in soy and wine, then lightly dry off with some of the mixed flours. Add the egg yolks, mix through to coat all the meat, then roll each piece of pork into the remaining flours. Put aside.
3. Mix 'C' ingredients into a bowl. Mix thickening in another bowl.

Cooking:
1. Deep-fry the pork pieces in a moderate hot oil until crisp and light golden (4 minutes) dropping them into the oil separately and cooking in three batches. Remove with skimmer and drain on paper towels. Turn up the heat to smoking, then re-fry, this time, all the meat can go in together. Deep-fry 1-2 minutes. Drain and put aside.
2. Drain off the oil, and wash the wok. Heat 3 tablespoons oil to moderate and stir-fry the capsicums and onion until they are slightly softened (1-2 minutes). Be careful you do no scorch or overcook them. Add carrot, pineapple and pickles and stir through quickly to combine.
3. Pour in the sauce stirring into centre of the wok for 30 seconds, then add thickening, stirring until sauce is thickened to a holding consistency.
4. Return the pork pieces and 'marry' all the ingredients over high heat. When the sauce coats and clings to the meat, serve immediately.
5. Once the flour and the egg yolks have been applied to the meat you must proceed with the deep-frying soon after, otherwise the juices of the meat begin to penetrate the flour and the coating will fall off. If you want to prepare this early, complete the first deep-frying and fry the second time just before you cook the vegetables.

Barbecue Roast Pork or Pork Sparerib

The Cantonese make the best roast meats and barbecue roast pork is always a favourite. It is versatile, as it is equally good hot or cold, makes a tasty tidbit, or horsd'oeuvres with drinks, or can be served as an important dinner dish. It combines well with other meats and vegetables in stir-fried dishes and with chopped spring onions I can recommend it as a super sandwich filling.

You will need:
1 kg (2 lb) piece of pork, shoulder, fillet or belly
  or 1 kg (2lb) spareribs

Marinade for pork: mix in a bowl
2 cloves crushed garlic
3 slices ginger
1 teaspoon sugar
1/4 teaspoon five-spice powder
1/4 teaspoon white pepper
Tiniest pinch red food colouring, giving the characteristic pinkish
  bronze colour
2 tablespoons hoi sin sauce
1 tablespoon Chinese (Shaohsing) rice wine
1/2 tablespoon dark soy
1/2 tablespoon light soy

Preparation:
1. Cut the pork into steaks approximately 4 cm (1 1/2 inches) thick and add to marinade. Turn the pork in marinade sauce occasionally. Marinate 4-6 hours.

Cooking:
1. Heat the oven to 180°C (355°F). Place the pork pieces on a cake rack in the middle of the oven. Place a pan with 5 mm (1/4 inch) of water on the bottom rack in the oven. Roast 30 minutes.

> *Points of interest:*
> Don't place your meat in a roasting pan, you won't get the same result. The small amount of water in the pan at the bottom of the oven will keep the pork from drying out and also catches juices from the meat. If you have too much water or if the water is too close to the meat, you will have a 'steaming' effect on the pork. I admit, you have an oven rack to wash afterwards, but at least there is no spitting of fat on the sides of the oven.

Sweet and Sour Pork
(plate from the "Gifthouse"
Hawthorn, Victoria) - page 79

**Beijing (Peking)
Beef - page 86**

Bean Curd and
Vegetables - page 99

Curry Puffs - page 107

Steamed Spareribs in Chilli and Black Bean Sauce

Ingredients:
500 g spareribs
2 tablespoons black beans
1 teaspoon sugar
1/4 teaspoon salt
2 tablespoons chicken stock
2 tablespoons Chinese (Shaohsing) rice wine
2 tablespoons light soy sauce
2 tablespoons cornflour
1 fresh red chilli pepper, chopped
2 tablespoons chopped fresh coriander
2 cloves garlic, chopped

Preparation:
1. Chop spareribs through in sections.
2. Rinse black beans in a little water then chop roughly.

Cooking:
1. Heat 2 tablespoons oil in a hot wok and stir-fry black beans gently with salt and sugar for 10 seconds, then add chicken stock, wine and light soy sauce and simmer together for 30 seconds.
2. Remove the sauce to a mixing bowl and blend in spareribs to marinate for a least 30 minutes.
3. Add cornflour, mix well through the spareribs, then place ribs on a plate ready for steaming.
4. Spinkle all over with the red chilli peppers, garlic and chopped coriander, and steam for 1 hour.
5. Arrange the ribs in small dishes or serve them in small bamboo steamer baskets.

Pepper Steak

You will need:
500 g (1 lb) eye fillet
1 tablespoon oil

Extra:
4 tablespoons oil for frying

Marinade for beef: mix together in a small bowl
1/2 tablespoon finely shredded ginger
1 tablespoon light soy sauce
1 tablespoon Chinese (Shaohsing) rice wine
1/2 teaspoon sugar
1/4 teaspoon salt
1/4 teaspoon freshly ground black pepper
1/2 tablespoon hoi sin sauce
1/2 teaspoon chilli sauce

Preparation:
1. Stand the fillets in the marinade for 30 minutes, then work in 1 tablespoon oil.

Cooking:
1. Heat 4 tablespoons of oil in the hot wok and fry steaks in moderate heat for 3 minutes. Remove and slice into 5mm (1/4 inch) slices.

> **Points of interest:**
> Chinese recipes should not be altered to suit Western ideas to the extent that they are no longer authentic, they become neither one nor the other, but I think Chinese and Western dishes can often complement each other.

Fillet Mignon and Snow Peas

You will need:
4 slices eye fillet 1 cm (1/2 inch) thick
250 g (8 oz) snow peas or any green vegetable
Sprinkling of salt & sugar
65 ml (1/3 cup) water
Oil for deep frying

Marinade 1:
2 slices fresh ginger 5 mm (1/2 inch) thick
1 stalk spring onion, 2.5 cm (1 inch) lengths
3 tablespoons Chinese (Shaosing) rice wine

Marinade 2:
1 tablespoon light soy sauce
2 teaspoons cornflour
1 teaspoon plain flour
1/2 teaspoon pepper

Sauce: Mix in a bowl
1/2 tablespoon light soy
1/2 tablespoon tomato sauce
1/2 tablespoon Worcestershire sauce
1 tablespoon sugar
1/2 teaspoon cornflour in 1 tablespoon water

Preparation:
1. Bruise ginger and spring onions with flat part of chopper. Add wine. Marinate steaks for 30 minutes.
2. Add Marinade 2 for another 2 hours.

Cooking:
1. Heat oil in the wok to moderate and deep-fry fillet steaks for 2 minutes. Drain and remove to a plate. Pour off oil from the wok leaving 1 tablespoon behind.
2. Slightly heat the 1 tablespoon of oil left in the wok, stir in sauce until thickened, return steaks to coat well in sauce for 1 minute, then remove.
3. Heat 2 tablespoons of oil to just smoking, add salt, snow peas, sauté slightly. Add sugar and water, cover and cook for 2 minutes. Arrange snow peas to garnish.

Mango Beef

You will need:
450 g rump or fillet steak
2 stalks spring onions, cut into 5 cm (2 inch) lengths
2 firm ripe mangoes
Peanut oil

Seasoning sauce: mix in a bowl
2 teaspoons light soy sauce
2 teaspoons dark soy sauce
2 tablespoons vinegar
2 tablespoons sugar
2 teaspoons cornflour

Marinade for steak:
1 tablespoon light soy sauce
½ tablespoon Chinese (Shaohsing) rice wine
2 teaspoons cornflour

Preparation:
1. Slice steak into 5 mm (¼ inch) thick by 5 cm (2 inch) long strips, and marinate while you prepare the remaining ingredients. Slice off the two cheeks of the mangoes, and cut into thick slices.

Cooking:
1. Stir-fry beef slices in moderately hot oil. Drain and remove to a plate.
2. In remaining oil in the wok, gently sauté the spring onions, the stir in the seasoning sauce.
3. Add mango slices to warm through, then lastly return beef slices to combine.

Spicy Ginger Beef

You will need:
500 g (1 lb) rump or fillet steak
1 tablespoon fresh ginger, finely shredded
1 large clove minced garlic
1 small red capsicum
1 small green capsicum
4 tablespoons peanut oil

Marinade for beef:
1/2 teaspoon salt
1/4 teaspoon pepper
1 egg, lightly beaten
2 tablespoons cornflour

Sauce: mix in a bowl
2 tablespoons water
1 tablespoon light soy
1 tablespoon dark soy
1 tablespoon Chinese (Shaohsing) rice wine
1 teaspoon sugar
1 teaspoon chilli oil
1 tablespoon hoi sin sauce

Garnish:
1 stalk spring onion, cut into 5 cm (2 inch) lengths

Preparation:
1. Thinly slice the beef across the grain, then slice into shreds. Add to the marinade and mix well.
2. Slice capsicum into julienne strips and mix the sauce in a bowl.

Cooking:
1. In a hot wok, heat 4 tablespoons of oil until smoking. Add the beef shreds and stir-fry 1-2 minutes (until colour changes). Remove beef to a plate. Drain off oil, leaving 2 tablespoons of oil in the pan.
2. Add ginger and garlic for about 10 seconds, then add capsicum, stir-fry 1-2 minutes, then stir in sauce.
3. Return the beef shreds to the wok, combining thoroughly over high heat for another minute, then add spring onions. Serve immediately.

Anise Beef

This dish can be eaten hot or cold. If you wish to serve it cold, leave the piece of beef to stand in the pot until it is cook, then refrigerate and carve into thin slices. For a hot meat dish, slice the beef very finely, arrange in overlapping fashion on a plate an spoon over some of the hot sauce in which it was cooked.

You will need:
1 kg (2 lb) gravy beef, in one piece (shin beef)
Enough water to cover beef, 1 litre (about 4 cups)
65 ml (1/4 cup) dark soy sauce
1 tablespoon Chinese (Shaohsing) rice wine
1 tablespoon sugar
1 knob ginger, size of small walnut
1 clove star anise
1/4 tablespoon sesame oil

Cooking:
1. Place the piece of beef and water into a saucepan and bring to the boil over high heat. Remove the scum as it rises to the surface.
2. Add all the other ingredients except sesame oil and simmer the beef for 2 1/2 hours. You should have the lid only half covering the pot, so that in the cooking time much of the liquid will have evaporated and there should be about a cup or so of liquid left. If there is more then remove the lid completely and cook over high heat until it is reduced. Add sesame oil and simmer a further 10 minutes.

Asparagus, Champignons with Beef

You will need:
1 can (small) champignons
500 g (1 lb) asparagus
 (using tips and tender parts only)
250 g (8 oz) steak (rump or fillet)
4 tablespoons oil
1/2 teaspoon salt
1 tablespoon oyster sauce

Marinade for beef:
1/2 tablespoon light soy sauce
1/2 tablespoon Chinese (Shaohsing) rice wine
1 teaspoon sugar
2 teaspoons cornflour

Preparation:
1. Slice the beef thinly and marinate with soy sauce, sugar, wine and cornflour.
2. Slice asparagus into 7.5 cm (3 inch) lengths and plunge in pot of boiling water for 1 minute. Rinse immediately under cold water and drain.
3. Drain champignons. If large ones, slice in two.

Cooking:
1. Heat the oil in the wok, when smoking add beef slices and stir-fry. When colour changes (1 minute) sprinkle in salt, add champignons and asparagus.
2. Toss well until flavours are intermingled, add 1 tablespoon oyster sauce and serve immediately.

Beijing (Peking) Beef

You will need:
250 g (8 oz) rump or fillet steak
½ egg white
2 teaspoons cornflour ⎫ mix together
¼ teaspoon salt ⎭
Oil for deep-frying
2 cloves garlic
2 thin slices ginger
1 medium-large green capsicum, cut into julienne strips
1 small red capsicum, cut into julienne strips
1 red hot chilli pepper, chopped
1 cup bamboo shoots, cut into julienne strips
2 spring onions, shredded

Seasoning:
½ tablespoon dark soy sauce
½ tablespoon light soy sauce
2 teaspoons vinegar
1 teaspoon sugar
1 tablespoon Chinese (Shaohsing) rice wine
½ teaspoon sesame oil

Preparation:
Cut the beef across the grain into slices 5 mm (¼ inch) thick, then cut each slice into 5 mm (¼ inch) wide julienne strips.

Cooking:
1. Dip the beef strips into egg white and cornflour mix. Deep-fry in moderately hot oil until beef changes colour. Remove, drain and put aside. Drain off the oil and wash the wok.
2. Heat 3 tablespoons of oil in a hot wok, stir-fry ginger, garlic and hot hillies 1 minute (do not breathe the fumes as the chillies are cooking - or you will have a nice coughing fit). Add slivered capsicums and bamboo shoots tossing together for 2 minutes, then add spring onions. Stir in the seasoning, return the beef slices to combine with the vegetables and the seasoning for another minute and serve immediately.

> ***Points of interest:***
> This is a popular dish with my Australian friends as they appreciate the full-bodies flavour of the beef and the spicy seasoning. An added touch is to serve it on a sizzling plate. These are imported from Taiwan and are available at many stores.

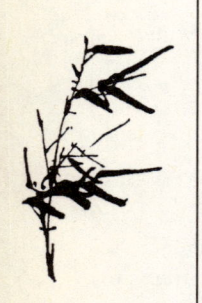

Beef and Tomatoes

I have often been asked if tomatoes, potatoes or peas are Chinese. My reply is: Are they Australian? All food, if it is fresh, is good for eating and can be cooked 'in Chinese'.

I remember this was a favourite dish of my grandmother's. I cannot swear that she cooked it in her home village in Canton, but I do know she cooked it often for us here in Australia, so that makes it Chinese enough for me.

You will need:
6 medium ripe tomatoes
1 white onion
315 g (10 oz) minced beef (rump) or minced pork
2 whole cloves garlic
3 tablespoons peanut oil
2 teaspoons sugar
1/2 teaspoon salt
1/2 teaspoon pepper
2 stalks spring onions

Preparation:
1. Roughly cut tomatoes into quarters.
2. Slice onion.
3. Cut spring onions into 4 cm (1(inch) lengths.

Cooking:
1. Heat the oil in the wok or saucepan, add salt and garlic and gently sizzle (don't burn the garlic). Add onions, lightly fry 1 minute then add minced beef. Toss quickly over high heat until the meat changes colour, add tomatoes and toss well.
2. Add sugar and pepper, cover with lid and simmer 6-7 minutes.
3. Toss through spring onions and serve.

> *Points of interest*:
> Served with a bowl of steamed rice this makes a quick meal that I have found useful for people on the run.

Beef and Oysters in Lettuce Parcels

A traditional dish that uses Chinese dried oysters, which are soaked until soft, then finely minced with the chopper. These are very expensive, but the flavour is extremely powerful and a little goes a long way. Most Westerners prefer the smoked oysters available in supermarkets.

The filling is spooned into crisp cups of lettuce, rolled up and eaten with the fingers. The fresh lettuce is a beautiful contrast to the soft rich filling of the oysters and beef.

You will need:
250 g (8 oz) finely minced rump steak
125 g (4 oz) smoked oysters or 4 Chinese dried oysters, soaked 1 hour in warm water, drained and finely chopped
½ cup water chestnuts, finely chopped
1 tablespoon oyster sauce
3 tablespoons oil
6 good lettuce leaves, edges trimmed with a pair of scissors to make the same size

Marinade for beef:
2 teaspoons light soy
2 teaspoons Chinese (Shaohsing) rice wine
1 teaspoon cornflour

Thickening:
1 teaspoon cornflour dissolved in 2 teaspoons water

Preparation:
1. Wash the lettuce leaves under cold water, dry off, trim and place in the refrigerator.
2. Add marinade to the beef and work through with the fingers to combine. Add water chestnuts.

Cooking:
1. Heat the oil in the wok to moderate heat, and stir-fry meat until colour changes (2 minutes). Turn up heat and cook until most of the liquid has been reduced. Add the oysters and oyster sauce. Stir for another minute until you have a clear, light glazed effect. Stir in thickening until boiling.
2. Spoon equal amounts into each lettuce cup and serve.

Beef and Onions in Oyster Sauce

Beef perfectly timed and seasoned is always hard to beat and should be a winner with Australians. Quality makes a statement of its own and shows through in a simple dish like this. You might serve it with a stunning dish of green vegetables like stir-fried snow peas or broccoli and of course perfectly steamed rice.

You will need:
500g (1 lb) fillet steak or best quality rump steak
$^1/_2$ egg white lightly beaten
1 tablespoon cornflour
1 clove crushed garlic
2 medium sized white onions, sliced into rings
4 tablespoons oil

Marinade for beef:
2 teaspoons light soy sauce
2 teaspoons Chinese (Shaohsing) rice wine
$^1/_2$ teaspoon sugar
2 teaspoons sesame oil

Seasoning: Mix together
1 teaspoon dark soy sauce
1 teaspoon light soy sauce
$^1/_2$ teaspoon salt, $^1/_2$ teaspoon white pepper
1 teaspoon sugar
1 tablespoon Chinese (Shaohsing) rice wine
1 tablespoon oyster sauce

Thickening:
2 teaspoons cornflour in 125 ml ($^1/_2$ cup) chicken stock or water

Garnish:
2 stalks spring onions cut into 5 cm (2 inch) lengths

Preparation:
1. Slice the beef thinly across the grain into slices approximately 5 cm (2 inches) long. Marinate them, dip into egg white and dust with cornflour. Place on a plate with crushed garlic on top.
2. Slice onions and spring onions and place on a plate.
3. Assemble seasoning ingredients in a bowl. Mix thickening in a bowl.

Cooking:
1. Heat 2 tablespoons of oil and fry onion rings in moderate heat until just softened and translucent. Do not brown. Remove.
2. Add remaining oil to wok (you should have about 4 tablespoons of oil) and when slightly smoking, add the beef slices with garlic and stir-fry over high heat until colour changes (1-2 minutes).
3. Quickly add bowl of seasoning, stir though then return onion rings to combine.
4. Stir in cornflour thickening in the centre of the wok, until bubbling and seasoning is thickened and coats the meat. Toss in spring onions and serve immediately.

> *Points of interest:*
> Crucial timing and heat are the cooking secrets here.

Beef and Three Vegetables

You will need:
500 g (1 lb) rump or fillet steak
¼ teaspoon salt
1 clove garlic, crushed
1 tablespoon wun yee (cloud ear, fungus available in Chinese stores)
250 g (8 oz) beans, best quality
2 stalks celery, tender part
1 white onion
¾ teaspoon salt
5 tablespoons oil
125ml (½ cup) water

Marinade for beef:
2 teaspoons light soy sauce
2 teaspoons Chinese (Shaohsing) rice wine
1 teaspoon sugar
2 teaspoons cornflour

Seasoning:
2 teaspoons light soy sauce
2 teaspoons Chinese (Shaohsing) rice wine
1 teaspoon sugar

Thickening:
2 teaspoons cornflour dissolved in 65 ml (¼ cup) chicken stock or water

Preparation:
1. Soak cloud ear fungus in a bowl of warm water 20 minutes, rinse, drain and put aside.
2. Slice rump steak thinly into approximately 4 cm (1½ inch lengths. Mix well into marinade. Put aside on a plate with the crushed garlic and the cloud ear fungus.
3. Top and tail beans and slice diagonally slice celery the same way. Cut the onion into half, lay cut side down and slice each half into quarters.
4. Have seasoning nearby and mix thickening in a small bowl.

Cooking:
1. Heat the wok for a few seconds, then cook 2 tablespoons of oil over moderate heat until oil just begins to smoke. Add ½ teaspoon salt, cook for 30 seconds then add vegetables to the wok. Toss in the hot oil for 1-2 minutes, until vegetables are glazed, then add 125 ml (½ cup) water down the sides of the wok (not over the vegetables) and cover with your wok lid. Continue to cook over high heat for 2 minutes then remove to a plate.
2. Wipe the wok dry, add 3 tablespoons of oil and heat to smoking. Quickly stir-fry the beef slices with garlic over high heat, turning constantly until colour until colour changes (approximately 1-2 minutes). Add ¼ teaspoon salt. Add cloud ear fungus, toss to combine with the meat for 30 seconds.
3. Return the vegetables to the wok and 'marry' all ingredients for another minute. Add seasoning. then stir in the thickening into the centre of the wok, until sauce begins to bubble and thicken. Combine the sauce with all the ingredients until the meat and vegetables have a smooth velvety coating. Serve immediately.

Points of interest:
Stir-fry dishes such as these must be cooked only just when they are about to be eaten. Get into the habit of preparing the ingredients beforehand as the actual cooking time is not much more than reheating time. There is, therefore, no point in cooking your stir-fry dishes early and sentencing them to die a miserable death in the oven!

Vegetables

Snake Beans in Sichuan Sauce

Ingredients:
250 g Chinese snake beans or slender round French beans
1 clove garlic, chopped
$1/2$ teaspoon ginger, chopped
$1/2$ teaspoon salt
1 small dried hot chilli, seeds removed and finely chopped
1 teaspoon Sichuan pickled vegetables (jar choi) finely chopped
80 ml water
1 teaspoon sugar
1 teaspoon light soy sauce
$1/2$ teaspoon dark soy sauce
$1/2$ teaspoon sesame oil
1 spring onion, chopped

Garnish:
1 tablespoon finely diced red capsicum
1 tablespoon finely diced Brazil nuts or peanuts

Method:
1. Top and tail the beans. Cut snake beans into 7 cm lengths, leave French beans whole. Deep fry in moderately hot oil until softened and just a little bit wrinkled (about 5 minutes).
2. Remove and drain.
3. Sauté the garlic, ginger, salt, Sichuan pickles and chilli briefly, then add the beans to combine quickly.
4. Add the water, sugar, soy sauces, and maintain a moderate heat while stir-frying. Continue until the sauce is reduced and the beans are almost dry.
5. Mix in the spring onion and sesame oil, toss well, and serve.
6. Arrange in a noisette on a round plate. Spinkle the diced red capsicum and nuts over the centre.

Asparagus and Crab Meat

A beautiful combination in stunning colour contrast and texture in this unusual dish.

You will need:
500 g (1 lb) tender fresh asparagus, rough ends snapped off
125 g (4 oz) can crab meat or 125 g (4 oz) frozen crab meat (available in Chinese stores)
4 prawns, deveined, washed and chopped into small bite-size pieces, marinated with a little salt, pepper and white wine and a dusting of cornflour
6 tablespoons oil
$1/2$ teaspoon salt, dash white pepper

Seasoning:
1 teaspoon salt
$1/2$ teaspoon sugar
1 tablespoon Chinese (Shaohsing) rice wine
1 tablespoon cornflour
85 ml ($1/2$ cup) water
2 egg whites, lightly beaten.

Preparation:
1. Plunge asparagus in a pot of rapidly boiling water with 1 teaspoon salt for 1 minute. Drain, rinse under cold running water to prevent further heating action, drain and rinse well and lay on a plate.
2. Mix seasoning together, add egg whites then add to crab meat.

Cooking:
1. Heat 3 tablespoons of oil in a hot wok, and stir-fry asparagus over moderate heat, adding salt and pepper for 1 minute (until heated through). Remove to a warm serving plate. Keep warm.
2. Heat remaining 3 tablespoons oil and stir-fry prawns until they turn pink and become bouncy (1-2 minutes). Arrange over the asparagus.
3. Wash the wok. Add crab meat and seasoning mixture, and stir until boiling and thickened (2 minutes). Pour over the asparagus and prawns.

Buddhist Heavenly Vegetables
(Vegetarian dish)

This is an interesting Buddhist dish called 'lohan tsai' (feast of Arahats) which features nine different vegetarian ingredients. The unusual flavour and textures of 'lohan tsai' are derived principally from the combinations of different fried foods. The traditional recipe includes dried bean curds, gingko nuts, tiger lily flowers, cloud ear fungus and fresh bamboo shoots. I have altered the combinations slightly to suit my palate, but it is still essentially an intriguing dish for vegetarians.

You will need:
4 stalks Chinese cabbage, bok choy
  or won bok choy
125 g (4 oz) bean sprouts
2 tablespoons dried cloud ear fungus
1 cup tiger lily flowers
1 cup bamboo shoots
1 cup water chestnuts
½ can lotus root
60 g (2 oz) transparent noodles (fun si)
3 tablespoons oil
1 teaspoon salt

Seasoning:
2 teaspoons light soy sauce
2 teaspoons oyster sauce
1 teaspoon sesame oil

Thickening:
2 teaspoons cornflour dissolved in
  65 ml (¼ cup) water (kept from
  soaking the tiger lily flowers)

Preparation:
1. *The dried ingredients*:
   (a) Cloud ear fungus: Soak 30 minutes in warm water. Rinse well to remove any grit or hard stems. Squeeze out water and put aside.
   (b) Lily flowers: Soak 15 minutes in warm water. Remove and save water. Tie a lovers' knot in each flower, this stops them from splitting into untidy loose strands during the cooking.
   (c) Transparent noodles: Soak 20 minutes in warm water. Drain and cut into approximately 10 cm (4 inch) lengths.
2. *The canned ingredients:*
   (a) Bamboo shoots: Drain, cut into 2.5 cm (1 inch) triangles (wedge cut).
   (b) Water chestnuts: Drain and cut each into half (horizontally).
   (c) Lotus root: Drain and cut into 5 mm (¼ inch) slices.
3. *The fresh ingredients*:
   (a) Chinese cabbage: Separate the stalks and trim off any wilted ends off the top leaves. Wash under cold running water and cut across at 1 cm (½ inch) intervals.
   (b) Bean Sprouts: Wash under cold running water and drain.

Assemble all ingredients on a large plate. Have seasoning and thickening nearby.

Cooking:
1. Add 3 tablespoons of oil to a hot wok, swirling around pan until just beginning to smoke. Add 1 teaspoon salt and stir-fry the cabbage for 2 minutes (reduce heat a little if cabbage starts to scorch). Next add cloud ear fungus, water chestnuts, bamboo shoots, and lotus root and stir-fry for another minute. Add bean sprouts, lily flowers and transparent noodles to cook for a further minute, then add 185 ml water saved from soaking the lily flowers.
2. Cover with the wok lid and cook over high heat for 2 minutes, then add seasoning. Stir quickly to combine through all the ingredients then make a well in the centre of the pan and stir in thickening until sauce boils. Mix well for another 10 seconds. Serve immediately on a heated dish.

Pork or Beef Stirred Cauliflower

I think many of my Chinese friends and readers will smile at the inclusion of such a homely recipe but I have often lamented that this attitude is responsible for the gulf that lies between Western and Chinese understanding of what our cuisine is all about. It appears that no self respecting restaurant would stoop to serve cauliflower cooked 'in Chinese' to their patrons. Is it too poor a relation to broccoli or snow peas? But cauliflower is a great vegetable when it is in season, so with no apologies, here it is.

You will need:
1/2 head medium sized cauliflower
1 green capsicum
1 white onion
1 tablespoon dried cloud ear fungus (available in Chinese stores)
250 g (8 oz) pork fillet or rump steak
1 teaspoon salt
1/4 tablespoon light soy sauce

A little cornflour
4 tablespoons oil
1 teaspoon sugar
185 ml water

Thickening:
2 teaspoons cornflour in 65 ml (1/4 cup) water

Preparation:
1. Slice the pork or beef across grain thinly 5 cm (2 inches) by 2.5 cm (1 inch). Sprinkle with a little light soy and cornflour.
2. Soak cloud ear fungus in a bowl of warm water 10 minutes, rinse, drain and soak again in clean bowl of water another 10 minutes. Rinse and drain.
3. Cut cauliflower into flowerettes approximately 7.5 cm (3 inches) long. Slice onion into half then each half into quarters. Cut capsicum into 2.5 cm (1 inch) wedges.

Cooking:
1. Heat 2 tablespoons of oil in the wok, add pork or beef slices and fry over high heat 1-2 minutes. Add a little salt and remove to a plate.
2. Wipe the wok, add 2 tablespoons oil and 1 teaspoon salt, and stir-fry onions, cauliflower, capsicum and cloud ear fungus quickly over high heat for 1 minute.
3. Add 1 teaspoon sugar, then 185 ml of water down the sides of the wok, cover with the lid and cook on high heat for 3 minutes.
4. Return meat, combine well, then stir in thickening and light soy in the centre of the wok until bubbling. Toss to combine well.

Prawn Stuffed Bean Curd

(Yields 12 cakes)

Ingredients:
6 fresh bean curd cakes, cut each in half
Cornfour for dusting

Filling:
125 g minced fresh prawns
$^1/_8$ teaspoon salt
Pinch pepper
$^1/_2$ heaped teaspoon cornflour
1 teaspoon peanut oil

Sauce:
1 cup chicken stock
$^1/_2$ teaspoon salt
1 heaped teaspoon sugar
2 teaspoons oyster sauce
A little thickening
A touch of peanut oil
Chopped spring onions

Garnish:
Fresh coriander

Preparation:
1. Make a shallow well in the centre of each bean curd square. Sprinkle a little salt and cornflour over each.
2. Mix the prawns, salt, pepper and cornflour into a paste, and then lastly add oil to bind mixture smoothly.
3. Fill the well in each bean curd cake with the prawn mixture, bringing the stuffing neatly to the edges.

Cooking:
1. Bring oil for deep frying in the wok to moderately hot, then gently slide bean curds in, stuffing sides down. Do not touch the cakes for a few seconds until they are slightly set, then gently move around the wok to ensure even crispness and colouring, ladling the oil over the tops whilst cooking. Remove when the cakes are a light golden coloour and delicately crisp.
2. Drain off the oil, leaving a film of oil behind, then add the sauce ingredients. Simmer 1 minute, then stir in a little cornstarch thickening to make a velvety holding sauce. Finally, add a touch of oil and sping onions, and spoon over the bean curds. Garnish with fresh coriander.

Snow Peas, Straw Mushrooms and Pine Nuts

Snow peas are always beautiful and in this dish they contrast well in colour and in texture with the smooth, rounded little straw mushrooms. Pine nuts repeat the crisp texture of the snow peas.

You will need:
500 g (1 lb) snow peas, topped, tailed and washed
1/2 can straw mushrooms, drained
2 tablespoons pine nuts (available from specialty food shops and Chinese stores)
3 tablespoons oil
1/2 teaspoon salt
1 teaspoon sugar
1/2 teaspoon sesame oil
125 ml (1/2 cup) water or chicken stock

Preparation:
1. Roast the pine nuts on an oven tray in oven 160°C (320°F) for 15 minutes.
2. Assemble snow peas and mushrooms on a plate. Have seasoning and nuts nearby.

Cooking:
1. Heat the oil in a hot wok, add salt for 5 seconds and stir-fry snow peas and mushrooms over moderate heat. Be careful not to scorch the peas over too high a heat. Add sugar, toss them quickly, then add chicken stock or water. Cover with lid and cook quickly 1-2 minutes.
2. Add sesame oil, then serve immediately on heated plate, garnished with pine nuts sprinkled on top.

Bacon and Potatoes
(A Real Country Dish)

You will need:
1 rasher lup yook or thick bacon pieces
3 medium sized potatoes
1 tablespoon bean sauce (min si jeung)
3 tablespoons oil
A little salt
2 tablespoons chopped spring onions

Preparation:
1. Cut pork or bacon rasher across into slices 1 cm ($1/2$ inch) thick.
2. Cut potatoes into bite-size chunks.

Cooking:
1. Heat 3 tablespoons of oil in a saucepan and over moderate heat, stir-fry lup yook or bacon 1-2 minutes.
2. Add potato chunks and toss until coated with glazing of oil. Add a little salt then the bean sauce and toss over high heat until sauce clings to the potatoes.
3. Add enough water to cover the bottom of the pan 2.5 cm (1 inch), turn down heat and simmer 15 minutes. Serve garnished with chopped spring onions.

Cellophane Vermicelli, Ham and Cabbage

You will need:
60 g (2 oz) transparent vermicelli
1 cup ham, cut into julienne strips
2 cups English cabbage, cut into julienne strips
1 egg, lightly beaten
2 tablespoons oil
$1/2$ teaspoon salt
$1/2$ teaspoon light soy sauce
375 ml ($1 1/2$ cups) chicken stock or water

Preparation:
1. Soak vermicelli in warm water 15 minutes, drain and cut into 15 cm (6 inch) lengths. Place on a plate with the shredded ham and cabbage.

Cooking:
1. Pour the beaten egg into an oiled frying pan to make a thin pancake. Slice into fine julienne strips.
2. Heat the oil in a medium sized saucepan, add salt and cabbage and stir-fry for 30 seconds before adding the vermicelli. Toss to mix well for another minute or two, then add 375 ml ($1 1/2$ cups) chicken broth (from soup) or water, turn down heat and cook on low for 3 minutes.
3. Stir in soy sauce, add ham strips and toss to combine with other ingredients. Taste to adjust salt, if needed. Serve garnished with egg strips.

Shrimp Tossed Zucchini

You will need:
3 medium sized zucchini, small tender marrows, chokoes or Chinese melons can be used
1 tablespoon dried shrimps, soaked 30 minutes in warm water
2 tablespoons oil
½ teaspoon salt
½ teaspoon sugar
¼ teaspoon pepper
1 teaspoon sesame oil

Preparation:
1. Soak and drain the shrimps. Reserve water.
2. Roll cut zucchini.

Cooking:
1. Heat the oil in the wok or pan. When the oil begins to smoke, quickly stir-fry the shrimps for 10 seconds. Add salt, then toss in the zucchini.
2. Continue stir-frying over maximum heat until the vegetables are glazed. Add sugar, pepper and sesame oil and 85 ml water in which shrimps were soaked. Cook and cover over high heat 1-2 minutes. Serve immediately.

Stir-Fried Bean Sprouts with Celery

You will need:
500 g (1 lb) bean sprouts
1 cup tender celery cut into fine julienne strips
1 cup spring onions cut into 5 cm (2 inch) long shreds
2 tablespoons oil
1 teaspoon salt
½ teaspoon sugar
2 teaspoons oyster sauce
65 ml (¼ cup) water

Preparation:
1. Wash and drain the bean sprouts and arrange on a plate with the celery and spring onions.

Cooking:
1. Heat the wok, add the oil and just before smoking add salt, then the bean sprouts and celery. Toss over high heat for 30 seconds. Add sugar and 65 ml (¼ cup) water.
2. Cover with the lid, cook over maximum heat for one minute, then add oyster sauce. Toss in the spring onions and serve immediately.

Bean Curd and Vegetables

Bean curd is prepared in many different ways. it is an important part of the daily diet, as it is a rich source of protein yet inexpensive.

You will need:
4 squares fresh bean curd
Cornflour
4 hearts of Shanghai cabbage
1 cup water chestnuts
2 cups peas or snow peas
6 Chinese dried mushrooms soaked 30 minutes, stalks removed
1 clove garlic, crushed
4 tablespoons oil

Sauce:
125 ml ($1/2$ cup) chicken stock or water
2 teaspoons dark soy sauce
1 teaspoon Chinese (Shaohsing) rice wine
$1/2$ teaspoon sugar
2 teaspoons oyster sauce

Thickening:
2 teaspoons cornflour dissolved in 1 tablespoon water

Preparation:
1. Cut each bean curd square into 4 triangular pieces, roll lightly in cornflour.
2. Mix sauce in bowl. Have thickening ready.

Cooking:
1. Heat the oil in the wok and when smoking, fry bean curd on all sides until golden and delicately crisp. Drain and put aside on plate.
2. Heat remaining oil, add crushed garlic, snap peas, mushrooms and onions, stir fry another minute, then add $1/4$ cup water or stock to the wok, cover and cook for 2 minutes.
3. Return bean curd to the wok and add the sauce, stirring gently to combine well. Make a well in the centre of the pan, stirring in cornflour thickening until sauce is boiling and thickened.

Eggs

Pork Scrambled Omelette

You will need:
4 eggs
$1/2$ teaspoon salt, dash pepper
60 g (2 oz) minced pork, bacon, ham or salmon (canned)
125 g (4 oz) green beans or celery, finely diced
1 cup chopped spring onions
3 tablespoons oil
1 tablespoon oyster sauce

Preparation:
1. Lightly beat the eggs, salt and pepper with chopsticks. Add spring onions. If canned salmon is used, drain, flake and add into the eggs.
2. Place minced pork and diced beans on a plate.

Cooking:
1. Heat the oil in the wok, swirl around the sides and when slightly smoking, stir-fry pork or bacon for 30 seconds, add diced beans and stir-fry another minute.
2. Pour in the beaten eggs, tilting wok around and gently stirring with wok chun, (spatula), letting the uncooked centre run to the outside edges. Continue this way over moderate heat, turning sections over to lightly brown and softly scramble.
3. Serve the omelette with oyster sauce sprinkled on top and garnished with Chinese parsley or spring onions.

> **Points of interest:**
> Eggs are a great standby in every cuisine, in a Chinese home, an omelette is often the extra dish when unexpected guests drop in.
> Interesting angle - I use this recipe for making egg sandwiches (leaving out the beans or celery). It always wins praise and makes a change from the boiled egg filling.

Tea Leaf Eggs

You will need:
4 eggs
500 ml (2 cups) strong black tea (your own favourite brand of tea left over in your teapot)
2 teaspoons dark soy sauce
1 clove star anise

Cooking:
1. Boil the eggs for 6 minutes. Soak in cold water, then crack shells all over by rolling the eggs across the corrugated bench of your sink or by tapping shells with the back of a metal spoon.
2. Heat the tea mixture to boiling, add eggs (with their cracked shells on) simmer 6 minutes, turning to colour evenly, soak 30 minutes. Remove shells and you will see that the black tea has seeped through the cracks of the shells and the eggs have a lovely marbled effect.

Soy Sauce Eggs

You will need:
4 eggs

Sauce:
125 ml ($^1/_2$ cup) dark soy sauce
125 ml ($^1/_2$ cup) water
2 teaspoons soft brown sugar
1 clove star anise

Cooking:
1. Boil the eggs for 5 minutes then soak in cold water and shell.
2. Combine sauce ingredients in a small saucepan and bring to the boil. Add shelled eggs and simmer for 5 minutes turning occasionally to colour evenly. Soak another 5 minutes (lid is on pot throughout).
3. Remove, cut into quarters and serve on a small plate over crisp lettuce leaves. The soy sauce can be kept in the refrigerator for many weeks and can be used again. You can use it up for 'Black Satin Chicken', or you might even be inspired to use it in your own cooking, casseroles etc.

> **Points of interest**:
> Soy sauce eggs are usually placed on an hors d'oeuvres platter at banquet dinners, but you might find them a good accompaniment to your salads.

Prawn Omelette

You will need:
6 eggs lightly beaten with ½ teaspoon salt and a dash of pepper
250 g (8 oz) green prawns, deveined, washed and cut into bite-size pieces
1 teaspoon minced ginger
¼ teaspoon salt
6 Chinese dried mushrooms, soaked 30 minutes, stalks removed, cut into julienne strips
½ cup bamboo shoots, cut into fine julienne strips
1 cup spring onions, shredded
½ cup cooked green peas
5 tablespoons oil

Seasoning:
½ teaspoon salt
2 teaspoons light soy sauce
2 teaspoons oyster sauce
1 tablespoon Chinese (Shaohsing) rice wine
Few drops sesame oil

Thickening:
1 tablespoon cornflour dissolved in 125 ml (½ cup) water

Preparation:
1. Stir-fry the prawns with ginger and salt in a little oil for 1-2 minutes until they turn pink and become bouncy. Remove and put aside to cool.
2. Beat the eggs, then add cooked prawns. Assemble all other ingredients on a plate. Have seasoning and thickening nearby.

Cooking:
1. Heat 3 tablespoons of oil in a hot wok and when just beginning to smoke, pour in egg and prawn mixture. Cook over moderate heat, breaking edge of omelette with wok chun (spatula) and tilting the wok to allow the soft centre to run out. There is no need to keep the eggs in one shape. Continue to cook until the eggs are softly set, turn sections over with wok chun to slightly brown the outside. Remove to a warm plate and place over a pot of boiling water to keep hot while you make the sauce.
2. Add the remaining 2 tablespoons of oil to the wok and over moderate heat stir-fry mushrooms, bamboo shoots, peas and spring onions for 1 minute. Add seasoning, then stir in thickening. Spoon over the omelette and serve immediately.

Points of interest:
1. Omelettes make good home dishes, providing good value, particularly in China where there is much poultry eaten. Homestyle omelettes are simpler than this one, usually having no extra sauces to garnish them.
2. Chinese omelettes do not have a 'set' shape as the English or French omelette, as Chinese dishes are designed to be shared.
3. Don't overcook your omelette, the texture should be velvety even though you have slightly browned the outside.

What is Dim Sum?

Dim sum is a special kind of meal made up of delectable bite-size morsels of food and is served at mid-morning through to mid-afternoon in Chinese restaurants. It is enjoyed throughout China, but the Cantonese excel in these little snack foods. Dim sum literally means 'dot hearts', so these little dumplings and pastries must be so subtle and dainty, that they 'dot' the heart, but never 'hit' the stomach.

The little dim sums sit snugly in small bamboo baskets that are wheeled around (if the restaurant is large enough) for your selection. The waiter will obligingly lift up the lids for you and if you can't speak the language simply point to what you fancy. Never eat more than one of each of your choices - so you can sample a number of different dishes.

All over the world, there are traditional ways whereby people gather to meet in a happy convivial atmosphere. In England it is the English pub, in America the cocktail lounges and wine bars, in Europe the coffee house and in China it is the tea house, since tea is the popular national beverage.

Actually, to go to 'yum cha' is the same as to go to 'dim sum'. Yum cha means to drink tea. Innumerable cups of Chinese tea are drunk throughout and are said to aid the digestion; as an added bonus, Chinese tea keeps you slim as a bamboo reed.

Your teapot will be replenished constantly, but remember to turn the lid upside down (it's an old Chinese custom) when you want it refilled. Another old Chinese custom is to lightly tap the two middle fingers on the table as a discreet way of saying 'thank you'.

Spring Onion Cakes

Spring onion filling:
200 g spring onions, cut finely
50 g pork fat or lard
2 teaspoons sesame oil
1 teaspoon salt

Mix all ingredients thoroughly with the fingers

Dough mix:
600 g flour
200 g pork fat or lard
230 g water

For frying:
Peanut oil

Preparation:
1. Place in a large stainless steel bowl the flour and water, mix well. Add the lard, mincing through strongly with the palm of the hand until the dough is fairly smooth.
2. Sprinkle the working bench with flour and transfer the dough to the bench. Knead vigorously for 5 minutes until the dough is smooth and pliable.

Method:
1. Roll into a sausage about 40 cm long and break off into 4 cm pieces. Cover with a teatowel (the dough should be used as soon as possible).
2. Press down with the palm of the hand to make circles then roll each piece into ovals of about 20 cm long and 8 cm wide with a small rolling pin.
3. Spread spring onion filling down the centre on each oval of pastry (like a sausage roll), roll edge over to enclose. Roll pastry around like a snake, tucking one end into the middle of the other end, gently pressing to seal. Lightly flatten the cake.
4. Heat enough oil in a flat frying pan to a depth of about 5 cm and place the onion cakes into the oil when oil is warm-hot. Move the pan around (to prevent burning) as they are cooking. Raise heat now to high, continue to move pan around for another minute, as the pastry begins to bubble and crisp up. Flip over to the other side when cake has puffed up and browned on one side.
5. Cut each spring onion cake into four for serving.

Spring Rolls
(Yields 10)

You will need:
10 spring roll wrappers, available ready-made in Chinese stores
1 teaspoon salt
3 tablespoons oil
Oil for deep-frying

Filling:
2 cups finely sliced chicken fillet (cooked)
125 g (4 oz) green prawns, cut into small bite-size pieces
125 g (4 oz) minced pork
1 cup finely sliced celery
1 cup bean sprouts
1/2 cup finely sliced bamboo shoots

Seasoning:
1/2 tablespoon light soy
1 tablespoon Chinese (Shaohsing) rice wine

Thickening:
3 teaspoons cornflour in 85 ml (1/3 cup) water

Preparation:
1. Heat 3 tablespoons of oil in the wok, add 1 teaspoon salt and over high heat stir-fry minced pork for 1 minute, then add prawns to stir-fry for another 30 seconds. Add remaining filling ingredients and cook a further 2 minutes. Add seasoning, then stir in cornflour thickening. Allow to cool.
2. Spread 2 tablespoons of filling evenly across the corner of the spring roll sheet. Fold in sides and firmly roll up in envelope style, shaping as firm and as round as possible. Moisten the edges of the sheet with a little cornflour paste to seal the edges.

Cooking:
1. Deep-fry in moderately hot oil for 4-5 minutes. Drain and serve hot.

> ***Points of interest***:
> For cocktail size, cut the spring rolls in half and serve with plum sauce drizzled over.

Steamed Pork Dumplings

(Yields 32)

These are the little flowerpot dumplings that have grown like topsy to become Australia's top selling dim sim!

Sieu mais and chuen guens (spring rolls) were the first of the big family of dim sums to be introduced to Australia and the sieu mai was then christened dim sim (a Cantonese dialect pronunciation). Victorians are the most enthusiastic eaters of dim sims and have made them into Australia's great snack food. I have it on good authority that Australian's eat more than 4,000,000 dim sims every week! But here is the original version.

You will need:
1 packet won ton wrappers (approximately 32 wrappers per packet)
Locally made won ton wrappers are quite small and make 'mini' sieu mais. Shanghai won ton wrappers (imported from Hong Kong) are larger, 10 cm (4 inch square), and are available in Chinese stores. I use a 7.5 cm (3 inch) round cutter and cut circles from these for a perfect size.

Mince filling:
185 g (6 oz) fresh minced pork (should be fatty)
125 g (4 oz) prawns, green
1/2 cup water chestnuts, finely chopped
1/2 cup bamboo shoots, finely chopped
1 cup spring onion, finely chopped
1 tablespoon salted preserved turnip (choong choy), finely chopped
1/2 cup finely minced celery

Seasoning:
2 teaspoons salt, 1/4 teaspoon white pepper
2 teaspoons sugar
2 teaspoons light soy
1/2 teaspoon sesame oil
2 tablespoons cornflour

Preparation:
1. Mix mince filling in a bowl, add seasoning. It is a good idea to chill the filling for at least 30 minutes before wrapping.
2. Hold a wrapper in the palm of your left hand, place 1 tablespoon of filling in the centre of the wrapper, wrap the sides up and around squeezing the skin close to the filling. The top of the wrapper gathers naturally into pleats. Gently push the filling down from the top to pack the 'flower pot' firmly and top up with extra filling if needed. The filling should be seen above the wrapper. Flatten the bases slightly and place over boiling water in a lightly oiled bamboo basket or a lightly oiled plate or cake pan on a steaming rack and steam 15-20 minutes. Serve with a dip of soy sauce and sesame oil (2 parts soy to 1 part sesame oil).

> *Points of interest*:
> Aluminium steamers like the bamboo basket steamers are very useful for steaming Chinese dumplings. The bottom part of the steamer is half filled with boiling water and the first and second tiers are filled with perforated racks. You stack the dumplings straight on to these racks to steam.

Baked Pork Wraplings
(Yields 32)

This is a family favourite, enjoyed by four generations and included in almost all of our family celebrations.

You will need:
500 g (1 lb) puff pastry, rolled out as thinly as possible
500 g (1 lb) minced pork
1 tablespoon dried shrimp (soaked 30 minutes, then chopped finely)
1 tablespoon salted preserved turnip (choong choy), finely chopped
1 cup water chestnuts, finely chopped
$1/2$ cup spring onions, finely chopped
2 tablespoons oil

Seasoning:
1 teaspoon salt
2 teaspoons light soy sauce

Thickening:
2 rounded teaspoons cornflour in 85 ml ($1/3$ cup) water

Preparation:
1. Cut out rounds from the pastry about 6 cm ($2^{1}/_{2}$ inches) wide, use the water chestnuts tin 567 g size. Stack on top of each other and cover with plastic to prevent drying out.
2. Assemble all the ingredients together on a plate; have seasoning and thickening nearby.
3. Heat 2 tablespoons of oil in a hot wok to moderate heat, stir-fry pork until colour changes (1-2 minutes) then add the other ingredients to combine well. Add seasoning, then thickening and stir until sauce bubbles and thickens. Remove to a plate and cool.
4. Place a heaped teaspoon of filling into each round of pastry, close over by gently pinching edges together to make a half moon.
5. Pleat edges by pinching with thumb and forefinger. Brush with a little beaten egg to glaze and lay on ungreased baking tray.

Cooking:
1. Bake wraplings in pre-heated oven 210°C (410°F) on oven rung one above the centre, for 12-15 minutes, until wraplings are golden brown.

Curry Puffs
(Yields approx. 35)

You will need:
Filling:
1 cup potatoes (or sweet potatoes), diced
1 small onion, diced
250 g minced topside beef
2 cloves garlic, minced
1 teaspoon curry powder
Dash of sugar
Splash of fish soy

Puff pastry sheets and 2 inch scone cutter

Sauce:
1 cup water
2 teaspoons sugar
1 teaspoon vinegar
2 finely chopped red chillies
Pinch of salt

Garnish:
Finely chopped peanuts.

Cooking for filling:
1. Heat 2 tablespoons of oil in the wok and fry onions briefly before adding the beef. Combine the beef to fry with the garlic and the onions until the beef just begins to change colour, add the potato to combine for a minute or two then season with sugar and fish soy. Cool before wrapping.
2. Cut out circles of puff pastry with the scone cutter and fill each circle with a rounded teaspoon of filling. Fold over and seal.

Cooking:
1. Heat about 3 cups of oil in the wok, or in a large saucepan for deep frying. Over moderate heat, drop the curry puffs in one at a time and deep fry 3-4 minutes until golden brown.

Accompanying sauce for curry puffs:
1. Bring water and sugar to the boil, simmer together until the sugar dissolves.
2. Add vinegar, red chillies, salt and continue to boil over low to moderate heat as the sauce will thicken (30-40 minutes). Pour into small sauce bowl and garnish with finely chopped peanuts.

Crisp Won Tons with Sweet and Sour Dip

You will need:
1 packet won ton wrappers (approximately 80 wrappers, 250 g)
Oil for deep-frying

Filling:
125 g (4 oz) minced pork (a small amount of fat on the pork is desirable as it makes a smoother textured filling)
125 g (4 oz) green prawns, finely chopped
1/2 cup water chestnuts, finely chopped
1/2 cup bamboo shoots, finely chopped
6 Chinese mushrooms, soaked 30 minutes, stalks removed and chopped
A little egg, lightly beaten
3/4 teaspoon salt, dash pepper
1/4 teaspoon sugar

Sauce:
185 ml (3/4 cup) pineapple juice
2 tablespoons white vinegar
1 tablespoon sugar
2 tablespoons tomato sauce
1 tablespoon cornflour in a little pineapple juice
1 teaspoon oil

Simmer together 3 minutes, stir in cornflour until thickened and clear, then finally add oil.

Preparation:
1. Put all filling mixture in a bowl and mix well.
2. Place a small teaspoon of mixture into wrapper a little above centre. Fold into a triangle, pressing edges together to close firmly.
3. Bring the two opposite corners to meet at the back and pinch firmly to close, lifting the bottom tail of the triangle at the same time (looks like a nurse's cap). A little water or egg is sometimes needed to seal the edges together. Continue until you have made them all.

Cooking:
1. Make up the sauce, simmer all ingredients together and thicken. The oil gives a shiny appearance.
2. Heat the oil in a wok and deep-fry won tons until golden and crisp (approximately 2 minutes). Drain on absorbent paper and serve on platter with small bowl of sweet and sour sauce in the centre as a dip.

> *Points of interest*:
> It is a good idea to very lightly dust a tray with cornflour to hold the won tons when you are making them. The dough is very fine and inclined to be sticky, especially in hot weather. Teach your family to make them with you and freeze them, stacking them separately so they don't stick together. They are handy as appetizers with drinks.

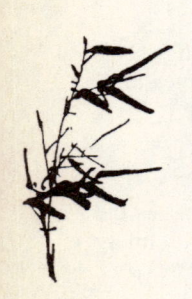

Sesame Prawn Toast
(Yields 24)

You will need:
6 slices stale white bread (toast bread is good), crusts trimmed off and cut into quarters or halves
3 tablespoons sesame seeds
Parsley
Oil for deep-frying

Filling:
250 g (8 oz) prawns, green
$1/2$ cup water chestnuts, chopped finely
125 g (4 oz) pork mince (fatty if possible)
$1^1/2$ teaspoons salt, dash pepper
1 teaspoon ginger juice
2 teaspoons Chinese (Shaohsing) rice wine
1 egg white, lightly beaten
1 tablespoon cornflour

Preparation:
1. Devein, wash and chop the prawns to a rough mince mixture. Mix all filling ingredients together.
2. Spread mixture thickly on to bread squares making a smooth mound shape in the centre. Sprinkle with sesame seeds and press a little bit of parsley into the centre.

Cooking:
1. Heat oil in a deep-fryer or wok to moderate. Slide in bread squares, prawn side down and fry until light golden and crisp (usually less than 1 minute). Flip over the other side and fry 30 seconds. Drain on absorbent paper and serve hot.

> **Points of interest**:
> These are enormously popular at cocktail parties or as an appetizer before a Chinese dinner. Make ahead, freeze, if desired. There is no need to completely thaw them out for deep frying. I have quite successfully fried them earlier to a light golden colour, then reheated them in a moderate oven for 6-7 minutes.

Something Sweet

Sesame Doughnuts
(Yields approx. 18)

These are eaten throughout the year, but particularly at Chinese New Year. They represent good luck - something like our Christmas pudding idea!

You will need:
185 g (6 oz) glutinous rice flour, (or mai fun)
½ cup soft brown sugar
250 ml (1 cup) boiling water
Oil for deep-frying

Filling:
185 g (6 oz) sweet red bean paste, available in small tins
2 cups sesame seeds, for coating the doughnuts

Preparation:
1. Dissolve the sugar in water in a medium sized saucepan and bring to the boil. Remove from heat and stir in the glutinous rice flour a little at a time until the dough is firm and well blended. (I use a pair of wooden chopsticks for this and stir the rice flour in as quickly as possible.) The mixture is rather dry with the flour cleanly separate from the sides of the saucepan.
2. Turn dough out onto lightly floured bench and quickly and lightly knead for a few seconds. Roll out into a long sausage shape (using hands only) about 2.5 cm (1 inch) diameter.
3. Cut the dough into 2.5 cm (1 inch) pieces and cover with a tea towel. Roll each piece in the palm of the hand to make balls, then flatten either with the palm of the hand or with a lightly floured rolling pin. Try not to handle the dough too much.
4. Place 1 teaspoon of sweet bean paste in the centre of the circle, close dough around to seal and roll into a ball again. Repeat until finished, then roll in sesame seeds. (If the dough is a little too dry for the seeds to stick, then a quick dunk in cold water will help.)

Cooking:
1. Deep-fry in moderately hot oil for about 10 minutes until golden brown. It is a good idea to move the doughnuts around a little while they are cooking so they will cook and colour evenly.

Almond Cream and Fruits

You will need:
5 teaspoons gelatine
750 ml (3 cups) water
2 tablespoons sweetened condensed milk
1 teaspoon almond essence
Lychees, strawberries, Chinese gooseberries

Syrup:
90 g (3 oz) Chinese slab brown sugar
125 ml ($1/2$ cup) water

Preparation:
1. Dissolve the gelatine in hot water. It is easier to dissolve the gelatine in a cup and to add the hot water a little at a time. Transfer the cup of dissolved gelatine into a larger container, then gradually add the other two cups of hot water.
2. When cooled, stir in the condensed milk and almond essence. Pour into small individual sweet dishes (I use champagne glasses), place in the refrigerator to set for 2 hours.
3. The syrup: Bring to the boil in a small saucepan. Allow to cool, then chill in the refrigerator. Spoon 1 tablespoon of syrup over each almond cream dessert and top with some of the above fruits.

Banana Fritters
(Yields 6)

To include or not to include in this book? That was the question. After a little thought I decided they were so good, why not? We have traditional jazz, modern jazz - perhaps this is modern Chinese.

You will need:
3 medium ripe bananas
Oil for deep-frying

Batter:
185 g (6 oz) self raising flour, sifted
335 ml (1 1/2 cups) cold water
2 tablespoons oil

Preparation:
1. Gradually add enough water to the sifted flour to make a smooth holding consistency, then add the oil, a little at a time and mix well.

Cooking:
1. Heat the oil for deep-frying to moderately hot.
2. Cut the bananas into halves, dip each half into the batter and deep-fry until crisp and golden. Remove and drain on absorbent paper, dust with a little sifted icing sugar and serve with a small scoop of ice-cream on the side.

**Sesame Doughnuts -
page 110**

Eight Treasure Pudding (plate from the "Gifthouse" Hawthorn, Victoria) - page 113

Sichuan Spicy Chicken and Peanuts (plate from "Gabriel Gaté Cookware Shop" Hawthorn, Victoria) - page 134

Cantonese King Prawns - page 139

Eight Treasure Pudding

Ingredients:
2 cups glutinous rice (available Chinese stores)
1 tablespoon butter
2 tablespoons sugar
1/2 cup sweet red bean paste (available Chinese stores)
30 Chinese red dates (available Chinese stores)
10 Chinese cumquats (available Chinese stores)
Small handful of almonds
Small handful of glace cherries, red and green

The syrup:
1 teaspoon butter or oil
1 tablespoon sugar
1/2 cup fresh orange juice
2 teaspoons cornflour, mixed in a little orange juice

Method:
1. Wash the rice in water until clean, add same amount of cold water, bring to a boil, cover and cook over high heat until the water is absorbed. Reduce the heat to low, cover pot with lid and simmer for another 15 minutes. Remove cooked rice to a bowl, add 1 tablespoon of butter and 2 tablespoons of sugar, mix well.
2. Butter a 6 inch pudding bowl and arrange the dried fruits and nuts attractively to form a pattern on the bottom of the bowl.
3. Place 1/3 of the hot rice in the bowl, carefully covering the fruit and pressing gently and firmly, then spread the bean paste over the rice. Cover the bean paste with another 1/3 of the rice. Arrange more dates around the sides of the bowl. Cover with remaining rice, flattening to the top of the bowl.
4. Cover with 2 layers of foil and steam 1 hour. When cool, turn out.

The syrup:
Simmer orange juice and sugar until the sugar is dissolved. Stir in the cornflour mixture and pour lightly over the pudding. Serve immediately.

Coconut Rice Balls
(Yields 20)

You will need:
2½ cups glutinous rice flour
3 tablespoons cornflour
125 ml (½ cup) boiling water
1 tablespoon lard or margarine
2 tablespoons sugar
1½ cups sweet bean paste
Glace cherries for decoration
1 small cup coconut (desiccated)

Preparation:
1. Put the glutinous rice flour on to a lightly floured bench. Make a well in the centre and add the sugar and lard.
2. Put the cornflour into a bowl, and add the boiling water, mixing quickly to blend with a pair of chopsticks. Pour into glutinous rice flour mixture and knead together quickly and lightly. This is a fairly hard mixture, but you can add a little extra cold water if it is too dry to knead. The dough should be smooth and soft, but not wet.
3. Roll the dough out into a long sausage about 2.5 cm (1 inch) in diameter, and cut into 20 small pieces. Flatten each piece with the palm of the hand and place a teaspoon of the sweet bean filling in the centre of the circle. Pinch and pleat the dough to make a round shape.

Cooking:
1. Place the dumplings on a greased steamer or on a greased cake tin. Place on a steamer rack over boiling water and steam 10 minutes.
2. Remove and roll in coconut while dumplings are still hot. Decorate the top with half of a glace cherry.

Toffee Apples

You will need:
3 granny smith apples
60 g (2 oz) sifted plain flour
2 tablespoons cornflour
1 egg white, beaten
2 tablespoons sesame seeds
Oil for deep-frying
A little water

Toffee:
90 g (3 oz) white sugar
1 tablespoon lard
1 1/2 tablespoons water

Preparation:
1. Peel and core the apples and cut into 2 cm (3/4 inch) slices. Dust with plain flour.
2. Mix the two flours together and add the egg white. Mix to a thick smooth batter with a little water and dip apple slices into lightly coat.

Cooking:
1. Heat the oil in a hot wok and when just beginning to smoke deep-fry the apples slices until golden (about 2 minutes). Remove, drain on absorbent paper.
2. Pour off oil from wok and add sugar and lard to cook over a moderate heat. Stir with a wooden spoon until sugar is melted, then add water. Turn down heat a little and cook until mixture just begins to colour. Reduce heat to the lowest point and simmer until toffee is a golden amber colour. Sprinkle in the sesame seeds. Add the apples quickly turning them until they are coated with the toffee. Remove to an oiled serving plate. The apples are brought to the table with a large bowl of water and ice cubes. Each toffee apple is dipped in the iced water to set the toffee before eating.

> **Points of interest:**
> You should practise this recipe well before planning to serve them at your next dinner party. You need to be able to work quickly and confidently for success.

Sweet Bean Pancakes

The best Chinese pancakes I have tasted were in a superb Chinese restaurant in Pattaya Beach, Thailand! They're a little rich but I enjoyed them so much that I asked the chef to teach me how to make them. Here is the recipe.

You will need:
2 tablespoons oil
Oil for deep-frying
250 g (8 oz) Chinese sweet bean paste, any of these: sweet red bean paste, sweet black bean paste, sweet lotus seed paste
Coconut jam (kaya-malaysia)

Batter:
125 g (4 oz) plain flour
1 egg
185 ml (3/4 cup) water

Preparation:
1. Sift the flour in a bowl. Make a well in the centre and add the egg. Add the flour, mix lightly, then gradually add the water a little at a time until batter is smooth and creamy. Set aside.
2. Lightly oil 20 cm (8 inch) frying pan and pour in enough batter to make a thin pancake. Cook on medium heat until the underside is firm, then turn over to cook the other side for a few seconds. Remove and repeat until batter is used up.
3. Spread the sweet bean paste in the centre of each pancake and fold up into a flat rectangle. Seal edges with a little flour mixed with a little water.

Cooking:
1. Heat enough oil in the frying pan to cover the bottom well and fry the pancakes until delicately crisp and a light golden colour on both sides. Remove.
2. Heat the oil for deep-frying until just smoking then deep-fry the pancakes until crisp and bubbling (approximately 1 minute). Remove with skimmer, drain on absorbent paper and cut into slices to serve.

> *Points of interest:*
> Chinese pancakes are rather different from the Western idea of pancakes (they are definitely more substantial). The shallow first fry and the second deep-frying gives them a unique texture not associated with 'crepes'. I hope you enjoy them, I serve them with icecream, a non-Chinese touch, but rather good!

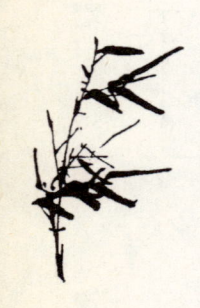

Homestyle Section

> 'To win the heart of your husband - satisfy his stomach.
> To uphold the love of your dearest ones - save them a good variety of food.
> To expect your children to grow strong - give them appetite.'
>
> *Confucius*

While the West counts its calories and worries about high cholesterol levels and fats, the Chinese are happily dieting and loving it! This section is dedicated to those who have truly learnt to love our food and now want to include it into the fabric of their daily lives.

Millions of people all over the world know that Chinese food is exciting, exotic and glamorous. It is all of that, but a Chinese family meal is a totally different affair. It is in the home that the very essence of Chinese cooking is learned, the secrets, the discipline, the devotion, a heritage steeped in ancient tradition. Unless a 'red-haired foreign devil' actually lives with a Chinese family, he could go on eating Chinese food in restaurants every day of his life and never come close to a diet that more than 1,000 million people are addicted to. He could be forgiven for thinking the Chinese exist on a daily diet of black bean crab, tiger prawns and sweet and sour pork.

For a start, you must learn that there are no courses in family-style eating as there are in banquet-style eating. The various dishes brought out together are planned to give balance and interest and must be seen as a complete picture, rather like a full orchestral company. There will be one or two dominant instruments, but the total sound is dependent on every instrument if balance is to be achieved.

You could have on the table, a soup (clear), a meat, a fish and a vegetable. The only individual dish is your rice bowl. Everything else is communal and this system is, incidentally, a natural media for teaching children valuable lessons in consideration and discipline. You eat a little of this, some rice, a little of that, some more rice and so on until you are satisfied. I might add that the meal progresses very quickly due to a minimum amount of conversation.

The system allows for great flexibility in meeting personal needs and desires. The sharing of food is a natural bond, more effective that polite dinner conversation. It also allows for the unexpected guest or two with cunning ease, the family simply eats more rice, the guests are impressed with your hospitality, and nobody goes without.

The evening family meal is always an occasion in every Chinese home There is great joy, great contentment in sharing the end of the day around the table. No matter how simple, the Chinese regard their meal as an expression of goodwill, of shared wealth, a gift offered with both hands. Therefore, no matter how humble the home, the meal is at once simple and grand and always served with dignity.

When planning fancy dinner parties, there are usually at least six different courses and at restaurants this can go as high as twelve. Home cooking calls for a more sensible approach and I usually plan only three or four dishes (including soup) for any number of people between four and eight.

So here are some typical family meals that you might like to try. Do encourage everyone to eat their Chinese dinner in the way it was intended, each member of the family with bowl and chopsticks sharing together the fruits of your labour of love.

Homestyle Menu 1
Steamed Rice	28
Winter Melon Soup	43
Beef and Tomatoes	87
Steamed Black Bean Fish	51

Homestyle Menu 2
Steamed Rice	28
Beef and Chinese Turnip Soup	40
Crisp Fried Garfish	59
Bacon and Potatoes	97
Pork or Beef Stirred Cauliflower	94

Homestyle Menu 3
Steamed Rice	28
Bean Curd and Vegetables	99
Lemon Chicken	73
Fresh Peas and Pork Ball Soup	47

Homestyle Menu 4
Steamed Rice	28
Red Simmered Fish	64
Chinese Cabbage and Bean Curd Soup	40
Cellophane Vermicelli, Ham and Cabbage	97

Homestyle Menu 5
Steamed Rice	28
Fish Soup	42
Shrimp Tossed Zucchini	98
Fillet Mignon & Snow Peas	82
Pork Scrambled Omelette	100

Homestyle Menu 6
Steamed Rice	28
Chicken and Asparagus Soup	48
White Cut Chicken with Ginger and Spring Onion Dip	70
Stir-Fried Bean Sprouts with Celery	98

Homestyle Menu 7
Steamed Rice	28
Chicken Wine Soup	45
Beef and Three Vegetables	90

Regional Cooking of China

'Eat in Kwangchow, dress in Hangchow, marry in Soochow, die in Liuchow.'
Chinese Proverb

This old Chinese saying covers the rules for an honourable and happy life. It decrees that the best food is to be found in Kwangchow (Canton), the finest silks come from Hangchow, the silk centre of China, the prettiest girls live in Soochow and very importantly, the best coffins are made in Liuchow (timber country).

It is not easy for anyone to accomplish all these feats, but at least most Westerners who enjoy Chinese food can please my Chinese ancestors almost every time they go out to a Chinese restaurant in Australia.

Vast, mountainous areas completely cut off some regions from others and for many years there was little contact between the people. Thus the Chinese developed their own cultures, their own dialects and their own styles of cooking. As transport systems improved from one region to another, there was an importing of new ideas as well as various foodstuffs and ingredients. In spite of this, each region still maintained its unique style of cooking and today, the cuisine of China is still strictly classified into the four great schools; northern, southern, eastern and western.

A Chinese from one province may be too proud to learn the dialect of his neighbouring province, but he will not hesitate to adopt a dish if he likes it enough. He will work some of his own magic on it however to make it local, the Cantonese steamboat is taken from the northern Mongolian fire kettle or hot pot.

In all regions, pork, poultry and seafoods are the principal meats; vegetables are an important part of the daily diet; bean curd, mushrooms, fungi, bamboo shoots, water chestnuts are all used and basic sauces are common to all regions.

Here are the four principal cuisines of China with what I hope is relevant and interesting information.

Southern School
Cantonese

The Cantonese school extends to those regions in the province of Kwangtung, of which Canton (now called Kwangchow) is the capital.

Cantonese cooking possesses the largest repertoire of dishes in China and must be regarded as the most refined and elaborate of all the styles. There would be at least two reasons why this is so. Historically, Canton enjoyed a former wealth and leisure, a legacy from early trading days that brought for many, a style of life both extravagant and refined and fine food was necessarily a big part of this era. To a larger extent, the cuisine is the natural product of the geography and the climate of the region. Because of an abundance of fresh food, the emphasis in Cantonese cooking is always on enhancing the natural colour, flavour and fragrance of the principal ingredients.

Quick cooking using the stir-frying method for vegetables and the steaming method used often for fish, retains these characteristics. The Cantonese excel in roast meats and are famous for their crisp roast pork, glowing roast geese and ducks.

The tea house, with its varied offerings of dim sums is at its best in th[e] Cantonese cuisine and is deservedly famous for these little dainties that 'dot th[e] heart', but never 'hit the stomach'.

It was during the mid 19th century, that the first Chinese immigrants saile[d] from southern China to the West, to the lands of 'the new gold mountain', t[o] seek their fortunes. Subsequently, entire families travelled out to join them an[d] a remarkable number of them now run highly successful Chinese restauran[ts] overseas. That is the reason why the world is familiar with Cantonese cookin[g] and the Westerner can be forgiven for thinking that all Chinese food [is] Cantonese food and all Chinese people look alike.

Eastern School
Shanghai

This includes all regions east and south of the might Yangzte rive[r]. Principal cities are Nanjing, Shanghai, Hangchow and Yangchou. Thes[e] regions are often referred to as the rice lands of China. The warm sub-tropic[al] climate and fertile soil irrigated by the great Yangzte river is responsible for th[e] numerous varieties of vegetables and fruits that flourish in the region.

Shanghai was for many years an international port, regarded as the city o[f] sin, with its infamous Bund bringing in shiploads of foreign sailors. Foreig[n] Concessions ruled over the Chinese and erected signs in Shanghai's parks an[d] gardens that read 'No Chinese and dogs allowed'. Such was the social climat[e] of Shanghai in the days before 1949, the home of the wealthiest businessme[n] in the world.

Today, Shanghai is the largest city in China, with a population of over seve[n] million: gone is the sin-ridden port, but an indefinable cosmopolitan feelin[g] lingers on in spite of heavy industrialization.

The cooking of these eastern regions favours much use of soy sauce in thei[r] long simmering red-cooked dishes, bean curd in various forms and mushroom[s] and vegetables are preserved and used very imaginatively.

Western School
Sichuan

Sichuan meaning four rivers is the largest single province of China[.] Situated on the upper reaches of the Yangzte river, it is an extremely fertile are[a] with crops of rice, wheat, corn and cotton, fruits and vegetables of ever[y] description. Although inland, it has no shortage of fish for it is endowed wit[h] many lakes and swiftly flowing rivers and streams. Sichuan is famous for it[s] fiery hot dishes, spiced with their locally grown little hot chillies and sometimes their fagara peppercorn. Take care when eating a dish with thi[s] pepper, on first tasting the dish seems relatively mild, but a short while late[r] the pepper begins to work and a peculiar numbness starts to spread in th[e] mouth. Apparently this strong spicing of their dishes is no deterrent, for ther[e] are many devotees of Sichuan food and in the West it strongly competes wit[h] the milder Cantonese food. Sichuan cooking however, is not limited to fier[y] hot dishes. They make good use of garlic, ginger and onions and I like thei[r] feeling for interesting textures. They use varieties of fungi to provide eithe[r]

crisp or feather-light contrast to a main ingredient and their silky smooth chicken and bean curd dishes are a real delight. Chewy, yet tender are their pickled jelly fish shreds and they cook their finely shredded meats in such a manner that they are dry, yet fluffy. Stir-frying is a technique commonly used, as it is in other regional cuisines, but there is a difference in that there is very little accompanying gravy or juice. Smoked meats are a speciality of the region, with smoked camphor duck a famous Sichuan dish.

Northern School
Shantung, Hopei and Honan

Beijing's Imperial Palace was a major influence on northern cooking, as China's greatest artists and entertainers with China's finest chefs were constantly being summoned from every region to serve the courts.

Further to the north lies Mongolia and it was inevitable that native dishes from that region have found their way to the northern capital. Northern China has bitterly cold winters and a great deal of the terrain is mountainous, so there is little cultivation of rice crops. However, wheat, barley, corn and millet are important, and the cuisine makes good use of these grains as flour for making noodles, bread and all manner of dumplings. Chinese cabbage, known as Tientsin cabbage, makes a daily appearance at the family table; many types of beans and root vegetables such as turnips and sweet potatoes are important contributions to the peoples' diet. Mountain sheep and goat are included in some meat dishes - although this meat is not favoured in other regions of China because of its strong odour.

Generally speaking, in its unadulterated form, northern food is plainer and heartier than any of the other styles, particularly Cantonese, but there is a purity of flavour and a non-pretentious characteristic that is pleasantly satisfying.

Beijing (Peking) duck is of course, world renowned and justifiably so. I think it owes much of its fame to the way it is eaten as much as to anything else. The dry pancakes provide proper contrast to the rich oily duck and the crisp succulent chestnut skin!

Regional Cooking
— Soups —

Fish Ball Soup
(Nanjing)

You will need:
2 litres (8 cups) chicken broth
1 kg (2 lb) fish fillets - pike, flathead, garfish
250 ml (1 cup) water in which you have added 2 teaspoons salt
1 teaspoon minced dried shrimps
1 teaspoon light soy sauce
1 teaspoon ginger juice, use a garlic press
Dash white pepper
1 tablespoon preserved Shanghai vegetable or shredded jar choy (Sichuan vegetable)
1/2 head lettuce

> **Points of interest:**
> Fish balls can be bought ready made these days.

Preparation:
1. Scrape the meat from the fish fillets with a metal spoon. Place on a chopping board and mince with the chopper. Place into a bowl and beat with the hand until it is a smooth, slightly stiff paste, gradually adding 250 ml (1 cup) water into which you have added the salt. Use the same action as the old-fashioned method of creaming butter and sugar together. Mix in dried shrimps, soy sauce, ginger juice and pepper. Scoop up 1 heaped teaspoon of fish meat at a time and shape into round balls. Put aside.
2. Wash lettuce and roughly break each leaf into two. You can use darker leaves as well as the pale leaves. It makes an interesting colour combination, but don't use wilted browned leaves.

Cooking:
1. Heat the chicken broth to boiling, drop fish balls in and simmer 5 minutes. Add preserved vegetables and lettuce leaves to cook a further 2 minutes, until just softened.
2. Ladle into a soup tureen, arranging the green lettuce attractively around the white fish balls.

Sour Hot Soup
(Sichuan)

You will need:
125 g (4 oz) pork meat, sliced thinly and marinated in 1 teaspoon light soy sauce, $^1/_2$ teaspoon sesame oil, 1 teaspoon cornflour
3 tablespoons oil
2 litres (8 cups) water
1 teaspoon salt
1 teaspoon sugar
1 cup bamboo shoots, cut into thin julienne strips
3 fresh bean curd cakes, cut into 1 cm ($^1/_2$ inch) julienne strips
2 eggs, lightly beaten
1 tablespoon cloud ear fungus, soaked 30 minutes and rinsed

Place into your serving soup tureen:
2 tablespoons white vinegar
2 tablespoons light soy sauce
2 tablespoons chopped spring onion
1 teaspoon sesame oil
1 teaspoon Sichuan peppercorns, available in Chinese stores; grind to powder
1 teaspoon chopped fresh or dried chillies or $^1/_2$ teaspoon of chilli sauce
1 tablespoon minced ginger
1 tablespoon coriander (Chinese parsley, cut into 2.5 cm (1 inch) lengths)

Thickening:
3 tablespoons cornflour dissolved in a little water

Cooking:
1. Stir-fry pork slices over medium heat in 3 tablespoons of oil in a soup saucepan. When pork changes colour, remove to a plate.
2. Add 2 litres (8 cups) of water to pot, add 1 teaspoon salt and 1 teaspoon sugar. Bring to boil, then add bamboo shoots, cloud ear fungus and cooked pork slices. Simmer 5 minutes.
3. Stir in cornflour thickening until boiling and the soup is of a velvety consistency. Add bean curds, then gently stir in beaten eggs until the eggs float in soft tendrils.
4. Immediately pour over the ingredients in your serving tureen and serve.

Regional Cooking
— Fish —

Fish Fillets with Spicy Sweet and Sour Sauce Dip
(Guangzhou)

You will need:
500 g (1 lb) fish fillet, rock ling, flathead, barramundi, gem fish, king fish
Oil for deep frying

Marinade:
1/2 teaspoon salt
1/4 teaspoon white pepper
2 teaspoons sesame oil

'A':
1 tablespoon oil
2 cloves crushed garlic
1 teaspoon minced ginger
1 tablespoon chopped spring onions

Batter:
185 g (6 oz) self raising flour, sifted
335 ml (1 1/3 cups) cold water
2 tablespoons oil

Sauce 'B': Mix together in bowl
2 teaspoons chilli sauce
2 tablespoons vinegar
2 tablespoons tomato sauce
2 tablespoons sugar
2 tablespoons Chinese (Shaohsing) rice wine
4 tablespoons orange juice
1 tablespoon cornflour dissolved in a little extra orange juice

Preparation:
1. Slice the fish across the fillet into 2 cm (3/4 inch) widths. Marinate for 10 minutes.
2. Gradually add water to sifted flour to make a smooth batter of a holding consistency. Stir in the oil and mix well.
3. Make up 'A'. Heat 1 tablespoon of oil in a small saucepan and over low-moderate heat, saute ginger, garlic and spring onions for 30 seconds then add 'B' mixture. Simmer for 2 minutes, stirring until the sauce is blended and thickened. Put aside.

Cooking:
1. Bring the oil for deep-frying to smoking point in the wok or deep-fryer, then reduce heat before adding the fish fillets.
2. Dip the fish pieces into the batter, shaking off excess and deep-fry, dropping the fish slices into oil one at a time. Remove when crisp and golden brown (about 2 minutes), drain on absorbent paper and arrange on a heated serving dish.
3. Heat up the sweet and sour sauce, pour into a small bowl and place in the centre of the serving plate with the fish fillets.

Sliced Fish in Wine Sauce
(Beijing)

I have included this recipe because I believe greater use should be made of our fish. Unfortunately, there are still a few people who can only picture eating fried fish out of shop. To miss out on other ways of cooking fish is to miss out on one of the joys of life! Cultivate a sense of adventure and discovery in your cooking and make the effort to include unusual ingredients such as cloud ear fungus; the dish is not truly correct if you omit or substitute given ingredients.

You will need:
300 g (10 oz approximately) white fish fillets, rock ling, gem fish, king fish, barramundi, snapper
8 dried Chinese mushrooms, soaked 30 minutes in warm water and rinsed
  or 1 tablespoon dried cloud ear fungus, soaked 30 minutes
Oil for deep-frying

Marinade for fish:
1/2 teaspoon salt, dash white pepper
1/2 egg whites
2 teaspoons cornflour

Seasoning: Mix together in a bowl
3 tablespoons dry white wine
2 teaspoons sugar
1/2 teaspoon salt
185 ml (3/4 cup) chicken stock
3 teaspoons cornflour

Preparation:
1. Slice the fish fillets into pieces approximately 5 cm (2 inches) square and marinate for 5 minutes.
2. Simmer mushrooms or cloud ear fungus in boiling water for a few minutes.
3. Have seasoning nearby.

Cooking:
1. Heat the oil for deep-frying in a hot wok until just beginning to smoke. Reduce heat a little, and add the fish pieces, dropping them in one at a time. By doing this the heat of the oil is not reduced too much. Deep-fry only 1 minute, the fish should be removed before any browning. Drain and put aside. Pour off the oil from the wok, there is no need to wash it.
2. Add seasoning to the wok, simmer until boiling stirring until thickened.
3. Return fish pieces and mushrooms (or fungus) and gently simmer for 2 minutes. Serve on a heated dish garnished with Chinese parsley (coriander) or spring onion curls.

Regional Cooking
Bean Curd, Vegetables & Eggs

Ma Po Bean Curd
(Sichuan)

Ma Po bean curd is hot with pepper, and the diced bean curd gives it t[he] slippery texture of a just set custard.

This is a late night gambling den of a dish, both soothing and stimulating [at] the same time.

Ingredients:
4 slices ginger
2 cloves garlic
185 g pork, minced
Crushed wild pepper
6 cakes bean curd, dices
2 chopped spring onions

Sauce A:
1 tablespoon mushroom soy
1 tablespoon chilli paste, mixed with 1/2 cup chicken stock
1 teaspoon red (Chin Kiang) vinegar

Sauce B:
1/2 cup chicken stock
1/2 teaspoon salt
1 tablespoon Chinese (Shaohsing) rice wine
2 heasped teaspoons cornflour
1 tablespoon light soy sauce

Method:
Deep-fry the pork mince then strain off excess oil. Add sauce A, boil and the[n] add bean curd. Add sauce B and finally stir in the spring onions. Place on serving plate and sprinkle with wild pepper.

Gingered Cucumber and Carrots
(Shanghai)

You will need:
1 cucumber
1 small carrot
1 teaspoon salt
3 tablespoons vinegar
3 tablespoons sugar
2 teaspoons minced ginger

Preparation:
1. Half peel the cucumber, slice lengthways, remove seeds. Cut into 5 cm (2 inch) long julienne sticks about 1 cm ($^1/_2$ inch) thick. Sprinkle with salt and let stand for 30 minutes, then drain.
2. Peel the carrot, cut into julienne sticks the same as the cucumber.

Assembly:
Place the cucumber and carrot sticks into a bowl, add sugar, vinegar and ginger, toss well, chill in refrigerator and serve cold.

> *Points of interest:*
> This dish can be served as an appetizer before the main meal.

Oyster Cakes
(Shantung)

You will need:
3 eggs, lightly beaten
$^1/_2$ cup chopped spring onions
10 fresh oysters
$^1/_2$ teaspoon salt, dash white pepper
3 tablespoons plain flour }
$^1/_2$ teaspoon baking powder } sift together
Pinch salt
65 ml ($^1/_4$ cup) water
2 tablespoons oil

Preparation:
1. Add spring onions, oysters, salt and pepper to eggs and mix well. Blend in water to sifted flours.
2. Combine and mix with the egg mixture. Leave to stand for 30 minutes.

Cooking:
1. Heat 2 tablespoons of oil in the wok until just smoking, add 2 tablespoons of egg mixture, making sure you include one oyster in it, and fry over moderate heat for 30 seconds. Turn over and fry the other side for another 30 seconds.
2. Lift out, drain on absorbent paper and keep warm. Repeat until all the egg mixture is used up.

Bean Curd Salad
(Yangzhou)

You will need:
4 bean curds, each cut into four dice
1/2 cup slivered spring onions
2 tablespoons light soy sauce
1 tablespoon white vinegar
Salt and pepper
1 tablespoon sesame seeds, toasted for coating
Cornflour for dusting
Oil for deep-frying

Preparation:
1. Dust bean curds in a little cornflour.
2. Put sesame seeds in a dry pan or wok and stir over low heat until golden brown.

Cooking:
1. Deep-fry bean curds in hot oil until crispy. Drain well and put into a salad bowl. Toss over all ingredients. Sprinkle sesame seeds on top.

> ***Points of interest:***
> It is best to buy bean curds a day or two before you want them, as they are easier to handle than when too fresh. Store them in the refrigerator covered in cold water. If you remember to change the water every alternate day, they will keep for up to 2 weeks.
>
> In Australia fresh bean curd is pure white, but can be different hues of brown, cream and white in China, depending on the different beans used in different provinces to make the curds.

Regional Cooking
— Noodles —

Cold Spicy Noodles
(Nanjing)

Cold noodles came as a surprise to me having been raised on the rather elaborate Cantonese noodles dishes which always had loads of beautiful hot meats and vegetables. However the smooth texture of these silky ribbons and the unusual flavours and combinations of textures were surprisingly good. I feel they have a place in our cuisine alongside other salads so often featured in our summer season.

You will need:
500 g (1 lb) flat ribbon egg noodles, available in Chinese stores
1 rather large cucumber, the continental variety is excellent
3 stalks spring onions
1 tablespoon finely shredded ginger
2 tablespoons Sichuan preserved vegetables (jar choy)
1 tablespoon sesame oil
1 tablespoon light soy sauce
1 tablespoon bean sauce (min si jeung)
3 tablespoons peanut oil
4 tablespoons toasted sesame seeds

Preparation:
1. Peel cucumber, but leave half of the skin on. Slice lengthwise, remove seeds, then cut into 5 mm ($1/4$ inch) julienne strips. Slice spring onions into 5 cm (2 inch) lengths, finely shred ginger and jar choy.
2. Put sesame seeds into a dry wok or frying pan and continually stir over very low heat until seeds are toasted. Remove.

Cooking:
1. Boil the noodles in a large pot of boiling water until just tender. They should take about 5 minutes but it will depend on the type you buy. Test after a few minutes, the strands should be tender inside, but still firm on the outside.
2. Drain and rinse under cold running water to arrest any further heating action. Drain well and mix a little oil through.

Assembling:
1. Place the noodles into a large bowl, add all ingredients, including all seasoning except sesame seeds and combine thoroughly.
2. Arrange on a serving platter and sprinkle sesame seeds on top.

Regional Cooking Beef, Pork, Lamb and Chicken

Tung Po Red Cooked Lamb
(A Northern Stew)

Tung Po, the greatest Chinese poet of the Sung Dynasty, is said to have created a great many Chinese dishes during his banishment from court. This dish is named after him, but whether or not he actually created it no one is sure. The dish is quite famous in Muslim restaurants - Hong Kong, Singapore, Malaysia and Indonesia.

You will need:
1 kg (2 lb) lamb chump chops
2 small sized onions
2 medium potatoes
2 small carrots
1 chilli pepper
1 slice ginger 5 mm (1/4 inch) thick
1 clove garlic
Enough water to come halfway up meat
1 teaspoon salt
2 teaspoons brown sugar
1 tablespoon soy sauce, dark
1 tablespoon brown bean sauce (min si jeung)
1 stalk spring onion, 2.5 cm (1 inch) lengths
3 tablespoons Chinese (Shaohsing) rice wine
3 tablespoons oil

Preparation:
1. Cut lamb into 2.5 cm (1 inch) cubes.
2. Roll-cut carrots and potatoes into approximately 4 cm (1 1/2 inch) lengths. Slice onions, remove skin from garlic, finely chop chilli pepper.

Cooking:
1. Add the oil to the wok, add garlic, ginger and chilli pepper, swirl around the oil until smoking, then add lamb cubes and stir-fry 3-4 minutes. Add salt, half the onions an sugar and stir-fry another 1 minute. Add soy sauce and bean sauce. Toss to combine another minute then remove to heavy pot, adding enough water to come half way up the meat.
2. Simmer 1 1/2 hours, then place the vegetables on top of the meat to cook a further 30 minutes.
3. Arrange the vegetables on the bottom of a serving dish, add 3 tablespoons wine and spring onions to the meat, and mix through and ladle meat on top of the vegetables and serve piping hot.

Shredded Pork and Leeks with Sichuan Pickles
(Sichuan)

You will need:
500 g (1 lb) lean pork
1/2 leek
3 tablespoons Sichuan vegetables (jar choy)
1 small hot chilli pepper
1 teaspoon minced ginger
1 clove minced garlic
4 tablespoons oil
3 tablespoons chicken stock or water
30 g (1 oz) cellophane noodles (fun si)
Oil for deep-frying

Seasoning: mix in a bowl
1 tablespoon light soy sauce
1 teaspoon sugar
1/2 teaspoon salt, 1/4 teaspoon pepper

Preparation:
1. Cut the pork, leek and pickles into thin julienne strips. Finely chop chilli pepper.
2. Deep-fry the cellophane noodles in hot oil, test temperature of the oil by dropping one strand of noodle into the wok, it should immediately puff up. Be sure you separate the noodle strands and fry only a small amount at a time. Remove, drain and put aside.

Cooking:
1. Heat 3 tablespoons of oil in the wok to smoking, reduce heat and add ginger, garlic and hot pepper to cook 10 seconds. Add the pork shreds, turning up the heat to a maximum and toss until the pork changes colour, then add Sichuan vegetables and mix through. Add seasoning and remove to a plate.
2. Add 1 tablespoon of oil to the wok and stir-fry the leeks for 2 minutes over low heat. Return the pork, turn up the heat and give it a final combination toss, adding 3 tablespoons of chicken stock or water.
3. Serve on a heated dish with the cellophane noodles as a garnish on top.

> ***Points of interest:***
> The hot pungent saltiness of the Sichuan vegetables has the effect of doubling the strength of the principal food with which it is cooked.

Beijing (Peking) Duck

The classic Beijing (Peking) duck recipe is not really suitable for home cooking, no matter what you are told. The skin is separated from the flesh of the duck by inserting a piping of some sort into the windpipe and blowing in air. The bird then puffs up and inflates like a balloon and a tight knot is tied around the neck to keep the air in. The hygiene of this practice is doubtful, both for the cook as well as the diner and restaurants now operate a pump either by hand or foot (like a bicycle pump) to do the job. Another criteria is an exceptionally hot oven (they have specially constructed ones in the East just for this dish). You also need experienced skills, and finally, the duck itself; should be a Beijing duck bred and raised specifically for this purpose. The Cantonese roast duckling however, is a good substitute, provided the bird is tender and plump. A good layer of fat underneath the skin is desirable, yet I have heard the uninitiated on introduction to this culinary masterpiece condemn the dish for this very attribute!

Beijing duck owes its fame I think, not entirely to the way it is cooked but to the way it is eaten. The skin is carved off the bird in about 5 cm (2 inch) square sections (a merest whisper of flesh may accompany it) and eaten wrapped in a pancake with a slice of fresh cucumber, spring onion and a brushing of plum sauce.

The second course consists of the tender meat, usually served up with green vegetables, the third course (or courses) are a variety of dishes cooked with the offal and the fourth and final course is a delicious duck soup. As a triumphant finale to the grand performance the head of the duck is brought in on a platter as affirmation that the guests have been given full measure! (I must say the only place I saw this done was in China). The rest of us may find the custom a little unnerving!

Pancakes for Beijing (Peking) Duck
(Yields 12)

You will need:
250 g (8 oz) plain flour, sifted
5 tablespoons boiling water
4 tablespoons cold water

Eating:
1. The skin of the duck is cut into squares of about 5 cm (2 inches) and placed in a pancake and brushed in a dip made of hoi sin sauce, a little sesame oil and a little sugar or plum sauce with a 1 cm ($1/2$ inch) wide julienne strip of cucumber and a length of spring onion 4 cm ($1 1/2$ inches) long. An electric knife would be effective in carving the skin of the duck.
2. The meat of the duck, simply chop Chinese style and arrange on serving plate over stir-fried Chinese cabbage (Tientsin cabbage, buk choy) or snow peas.

Preparation:
1. Sift the flour into a bowl, make a well in the centre and pour in the boiling

water. Mix through the flour quickly, the gradually add the cold water a little at a time until the dough is smooth but still fairly dry and manageable. Knead for a few minutes, cover with a damp cloth and stand 30 minutes.
2. Lightly flour a bench and rolling pin, and roll dough into a long sausage about 4 cm (1 1/2 inches) in diameter. Cut into 12 pieces, then roll into thin rounds.

Cooking:
1. Heat a heavy frying pan over high heat for 30 seconds. Reduce the heat to moderate and cook the pancakes one at a time in the ungreased pan. Turn over to the other side when tiny bubbles appear and they puff a little. The pancakes should be lightly speckled after about 1/2 minute of cooking on each side. Fold each pancake into a triangle shape, stack and keep covered with a tea towel. Serve at once or they can be wrapped in foil and refrigerated for use later. They can be reheated either by steaming, or warmed in the oven still wrapped in foil.

Shantung Potatoes

Shantung is a province of the north. Some say that northern cooking should be called the Shantung school of cooking rather than the Peking school of cooking.

The locals use a great deal of sauces on their table such as the salt and pepper mix, chilli and soy mixed together, garlic and vinegar, and ginger and vinegar mixture. Plum sauce is sometimes mixed with hoi sin sauce and made into soy jam. The people brought up in this area are accustomed to strong chunky, hearty food and prefer it to the food produced in the southern kitchens which they consider to be fussy and elaborate.

Potatoes are enjoyed in this region and are eaten the same way as any other vegetable, they are meant to accompany rice.

You will need:
500 g (1 lb) potatoes
1 hot chilli pepper
1 tablespoon chopped onions
2 tablespoons chopped spring onions
1/2 teaspoon salt
2 teaspoons vinegar
3 tablespoons peanut oil
1 tablespoon light soy sauce

Preparation:
1. Peel the potatoes and cut into 5mm (1/4 inch) scallop slices. Stack the slices and cut into 5 mm (1/4 inch) julienne strips.
2. Simmer the potato shreds in boiling water for 1 minute. Drain. Chop the chilli pepper and arrange with the potato shreds and chopped onions on a plate.

Cooking:
1. Heat the oil in the wok swirling around the sides, stir-fry the chilli pepper for 10 seconds then chopped onions for 30 seconds. Lower the heat and remove the chilli peppers and onions with a perforated spoon.
2. Turn up the heat, add potato shreds and stir-fry in hot oil for 2 minutes. Add soy sauce, salt, vinegar and spring onions.
3. Reduce heat and continue to stir-fry for another minute. Lift out with skimmer and drain on absorbent paper. Serve on a heated dish.

Sichuan Spicy Chicken and Peanuts

You will need:
2 chicken breasts, boned and skin removed
1 small red capsicum
1 small green capsicum
1 onion
1 clove garlic, sliced
3 slices fresh ginger

Marinade for chicken:
A little egg white
1 tablespoon water
Dusting of cornflour

Sauce: Mix in a bowl
1 teaspoon cornflour
1 tablespoon Chinese (Shaohsing) rice wine
$1/2$ tablespoon light soy sauce
2 teaspoons chilli bean paste, available in Asian stores
$1/2$ teaspoon ground bean paste, available in Asian stores

$1/2$ cup roasted unsalted peanuts
2 stalks spring onions - mainly white sections, cut into 1 cm ($1/2$ inch) lengths
peanut oil

Preparation:
1. Dice chicken, and allow to marinate whilst you cut the capsicums and onion.

Cooking:
1. Heat 2 tablespoons peanut oil in a pre-heated wok, and oil is just beginning to smoke, sizzle garlic and ginger for a few seconds before adding the onion and capsicums. Reduce heat to moderate, and stir-fry quickly for another minute, before removing to a plate.
2. Add another 2 tablespoons oil to heat, then stir-fry the chicken over high heat until the colour changes from pink to white (approximately 1 minute). Stir in the sauce combining with the chicken to absorb the flavours, then return the vegetables to combine, tossing over high heat for about 30 seconds. Stir in the spring onions and peanuts and serve immediately with steamed rice.

Beggar's Chicken
(Beijing)

The story is told that long ago an old beggar stole into the Imperial kitchen and successfully took off with a plump chicken. In order to disguise his prize, he wrapped the chicken in a large lotus leaf plucked from one of the many lotus ponds surrounding the palaces and covered it over with a thick layer of pond mud. At night he lit his usual campfire to warm himself by and placed his dinner in the fire to cook. The smells coming from his camp fire were so fragrant the trick was soon discovered and so was born 'Beggar's chicken'!

You will need:
1 roasting chicken, about 1.5 kg (3 lb)

Marinade for chicken:
1/4 teaspoon salt
2 teaspoons Chinese (Shaohsing) rice wine
2 teaspoons sesame oil

Stuffing for chicken:
60 g (2 oz) fat pork, shredded
6 slices ginger, shredded
2 stalks spring onions, chopped into 2.5 cm (1 inch) lengths
1 tablespoon sugar
1/2 teaspoon salt
1 tablespoon dark soy sauce
1 tablespoon light soy sauce
1 tablespoon Chinese (Shaohsing) rice wine
2 teaspoons sesame oil
2 teaspoons vinegar

Dough:
5 cups plain flour
1 kg cooking salt
435 ml (1 3/4 cups) water

3 lotus leaves, soaked 30 minutes in boiling water or substitute aluminium foil sheets

Preparation:
1. Wash and pat dry the chicken inside and outside. Rub the skin with the marinade and stand 1 hour.
2. Stir-fry pork shreds for 30 seconds, then add ginger, spring onions and all ingredients in stuffing ingredients. Stir for another minute. Stuff into the chicken, then wrap up firmly in the lotus leaves or the aluminium foil. If using lotus leaves, you should use string to tie the chicken up like a parcel.
3. To make the dough: Thoroughly combine the unsifted flour and salt into a large bowl. Ad the water a little at a time and mix through with your hands until you have a firm dough. More or less water does not matter, but a harder firmer dough is easier to handle. Roll dough out to about 2 cm thickness and completely encase chicken. Press edges together to close.

Cooking:
1. Place the chicken on a greased wire rack in the centre of the oven pre-heated 245°C (475°F) for approximately 1 1/2 hours.
2. Bring to the table, crack open the hardened casing with a mallet, open the lotus leaves and serve.

Red and Green Chicken Salad with Mustard Dressing
(Shanghai)

This vegetable salad makes an interesting change from the usual Western tomato salads with its bright colour and rather different salad dressing.

You will need:
3 medium firm tomatoes
½ bunch spinach
2 chicken breasts, cooked

Sauce: Mix well and chill
2 tablespoons light soy
1 tablespoon sesame oil
1 tablespoon vinegar
½ tablespoon mustard
2 teaspoons sugar

Preparation:
1. Slice the tomatoes 5 mm (¼ inch) thick, shred the chicken, plunge the spinach.
2. Arrange in separate sections on a plate. Chill. Pour over sauce just before serving.

Hot Diced Chicken in Ground Cashew Nuts
(Sichuan)

A Sichuan dish, although it enjoys considerable fame in Beijing. The ingredients are typically Sichuan, nuts and chillies.

You will need:
3 chicken breasts
Salt and pepper
3/4 cup cashew nuts
3 tablespoons oil
1/2 tablespoon cornflour ⎫ mix together
1 lightly beaten egg ⎭
2 teaspoons finely chopped dried chilli peppers

Seasoning: Mix in a bowl
2 stalks spring onions, cut into 1cm (1/2 inch) lengths
1/2 tablespoon cornflour
1 tablespoon water
2 teaspoons sugar
2 teaspoons vinegar
2 teaspoons light soy
1/2 teaspoon salt

Preparation:
1. Dice the chicken into 2 cm (3/4 inch) cubes, sprinkle with salt and pepper and mix with the egg and cornflour.
2. Mince the nuts roughly with the chopper or place in a blender. Don't grind them too finely.
3. Mix seasoning ingredients in a bowl.

Cooking:
1. Heat the oil until just smoking, and stir-fry the diced chicken for 1 minute. Remove to a plate.
2. Stir-fry the chopped pepper in the remaining oil for 30 seconds. Return chicken to the pan and combine for a few seconds.
3. Pour in the seasoning mixture and continue to stir-fry until well combined (30 seconds). Sprinkle in the cashew nuts, toss well and serve.

Chrysanthemum Crystal Chicken
(Sichuan)

I love to serve this chicken dish at buffet parties. It is completely made up the day beforehand (except for the turning out of the chicken and the garnishing). The chicken is juicy and sweet and the aspic and garnishes make it one of the prettiest chicken dishes that I know of. I love its name too, don't you?

You will need:
1 roasting chicken, approximately 1.5 kg (3 lb)
250 g (8 oz) smoked ham
1 teaspoon salt
65 ml (¼ cup) Chinese (Shaohsing) rice wine
6 teaspoons gelatine
1 litre (4 cups) hot water or very clear chicken stock

Garnish:
Yellow chrysanthemums
Small bunch of cherries or strawberries

Preparation:
1. Cook the chicken as written up for Hainan Chicken Rice (see Rice and Noodles). When the chicken is cooled, remove bones from breasts, and chop up into sections approximately 4 cm by 2.5 cm (1½ inches long by 1 inch wide). Cut ham in similar size and shape.
2. Lightly oil the bottom and sides of a deep pyrex type oval bowl and lay boned out chicken portions with alternating slices of ham on the bottom of the dish (the chicken and ham will be inverted later for serving). Line the sides of bowl with ham slices and build up centre of dish with remaining chicken pieces.
3. Put gelatine into a cup and add hot water a little at a time to dissolve and blend the gelatine smoothly. Transfer the dissolved gelatine into a larger bowl and add the remaining 750 ml (3 cups) of hot water. Ad salt and wine. Cool 20 minutes then pour over the chicken and ham in the bowl. Refrigerate for at least 2 hours.

To serve:
1. Just before serving, run a sharp knife around the sides of the bowl, place oval serving platter on top and carefully invert the chicken and ham.
2. Arrange a little posy of yellow chrysanthemums (or similar) at one side of the chicken and a bunch of bright red cherries (or similar) at the other side.

Cantonese King Prawns
(Cantonese)

Ingredients:
8 king prawns - shells and heads intact, but deveined and trimmed
3 tablespoons peanut oil
3 slices fresh ginger - size 20 cent piece
1 clove garlic - sliced
1 stalk spring onion - mainly white part, cut into 2.5 cm (1 inch) sections

Sauce: Mix in a bowl:
2 tablespoons Chinese (Shaohsing) rice wine
1 teaspoon sugar
$1/2$ teaspoon salt
$1/4$ teaspoon pepper
1 small red chilli pepper - finely sliced
4 tablespoons chicken stock
$1/2$ teaspoon sesame oil
1 tablespoon shredded leek

Cooking:
1. Heat oil in the wok until moderately hot. Sauté ginger, garlic and spring onions until fragrant, taking care not to burn them.
2. Add the king prawns to cook for 1-2 minutes until they turn pink and bouncy, then add the sauce. Gently toss the prawns in the pan to absorb the flavours then reduce the heat until the sauce has been reduced to about half. Add the sesame oil and serve garnished with shredded leek.

Chicken, Bean Curd and Salt Fish Claypot
(Cantonese)

Ingredients:
2 chicken breasts
100 g salt fish (dried variety)
2 tablespoons shredded fresh ginger
6 cakes fresh bean curd

Marinade for chicken:
2 teaspoons light soy sauce
1 teaspoon sesame oil
2 teaspoons Chinese (Shaohsing) rice wine
1/2 teaspoon sugar
2 teaspoons cornflour
1 cup chicken stock
2 teaspoons oyster sauce

Thickening:
3 teaspoons cornflour in a little water

Preparation:
1. Cut chicken breasts into 5 mm (1/4 inch) thick slices and add to marinade.
2. Shred salt fish and cut each bean curd into 4.

Cooking:
1. Heat 2 tablespoons of oil in wok and stir-fry salt fish, and ginger over moderate heat for a few seconds. Quickly add chicken and combine to stir fry until chicken changes colour.
2. Add chicken stock, combine together then transfer contents to the claypot.
3. Simmer 15 minutes, add oyster sauce, then stir in thickening. Serve straight to the table, garnished with fresh coriander.

Index

A
- Almond Cream & Fruits — 111
- Anise Beef — 85
- Asparagus & Crab Meat — 92
- Asparagus, Champignons with Beef — 85

B
- Bacon & Potatoes — 97
- Baked Pork Wraplings — 106
- Banana Fritters — 112
- Barbeque Roast Pork or Pork Spareribs — 80
- Bean Curd & Vegetables — 99
- Bean Curd Salad — 128
- Beef & Chinese Turnip Soup — 40
- Beef & Onions in Oyster Sauce — 89
- Beef & Oysters in Lettuce Parcels — 88
- Beef & Three Vegetables — 90
- Beef & Tomatoes — 87
- Beggar's Chicken — 135
- Beijing (Peking) Beef — 86
- Beijing (Peking) Duck — 132
- Black Satin Chicken — 66
- Braised Duckling with Baby Bok Chok — 76
- Buddhist Heavenly Vegetables — 93

C
- Cantonese Fried Rice — 29
- Cantonese King Prawns — 139
- Cantonese Roast Duckling — 74
- Cellophane Vermicelli, Ham & Cabbage — 97
- Chicken, Bean Curd & Salt Fish Claypot — 140
- Chicken & Asparagus Soup — 48
- Chicken & Mushrooms in Plum Sauce — 72
- Chicken, Shrimp & Mushroom Soup — 38
- Chicken Stock — 37
- Chicken Wine Soup — 45
- Chinese Cabbage & Bean Curd Soup — 40
- Chrysanthemum Crystal Chicken — 138
- Coconut Rice Balls — 114
- Cold Spicy Noodles — 129
- Combination Fried Noodles — 33
- Combination Soup — 44
- Crisp Fried Garfish — 59
- Crisp Skin Chicken — 71
- Crisp Won Tons with Sweet and Sour Dip — 108
- Crispy Prawn Balls — 52
- Curry Puffs — 107

D
- Dim Sum:
  - Baked Pork Wraplings — 106
  - Crisp Won Tons with Sweet & Sour Dip — 108
  - Curry Puffs — 107
  - Sesame Prawn Toast — 109
  - Spring Onion Cakes — 103
  - Spring Rolls — 104
  - Steamed Pork Dumplings — 105
- Drunken Chicken — 65

E
- Eggs:
  - Pork Scrambled Omlette — 100
  - Prawn Omlette — 102
  - Soy Sauce Eggs — 101
  - Tea Leaf Eggs — 101
- Eight Treasure Pudding — 113

F
- Fillet Mignon & Snow Peas — 82
- Fish Ball Soup — 122

	Fish Fillets with Spicy Sweet & Sour Sauce Dip	124
	Fish Soup	42
	Fresh Noodles with three kinds of Mushrooms	36
	Fresh Peas & Pork Balls Soup	47
	Fried Fish Rolls	49
G	Gingered Cucumber & Carrots	127
	Grape Cluster Fish	58
H	Hainan Chicken Rice	31
	Hoi Sin Chicken	68
	Hokkien Noodles with a Spicy Beef Sauce	35
	Hot Diced Chicken in Ground Cashew Nuts	137
I	Imperial Prawns	53
J	Jook	30
L	Lemon Chicken	73
	Lychee Mandarin Duck	75
M	Mango Beef	83
	Ma Po Bean Curd	126
	Meats:	
	Anise Beef	85
	Asparagus, Champignons with Beef	85
	Barbeque Roast Pork or Pork Spareribs	80
	Beef & Onions in Oyster Sauce	89
	Beef & Oysters in Lettuce Parcels	88
	Beef & Three Vegetables	90
	Beef & Tomatoes	87
	Beijing (Peking) Beef	86
	Fillet Mignon & Snow Peas	82
	Mango Beef	83
	Pepper Steak	81
	Spicy Ginger Beef	84
	Steamed Spareribs in Chilli & Black Bean Sauce	81
	Sweet & Sour Pork	79
	Tung Po Red Cooked Lamb	130
N	Noodles	
	Cold Spicy Noodles	129
	Combination Fried Noodles	33
	Fresh Noodles with three kinds of Mushrooms	36
	Hokkien Noodles with a Spicy Beef Sauce	35
	Noodle Salad	32
	Singapore Noodles	34
	Noodle Salad	32
	Noodle Soup	41
O	Oyster Cakes	127
P	Pancakes for Beijing (Peking) Duck	132
	Pepper Steak	81
	Pine Leaves Tea Smoked Duck	77
	Pork or Beef Stirred Cauliflower	94
	Pork Scrambled Omlette	100
	Pork Stock	38
	Poultry:	
	Beggar's Chicken	135
	Beijing Duck	132
	Black Satin Chicken	66
	Braised Duckling with Baby Bok Chok	76
	Cantonese Roast Duckling	74
	Chicken, Bean Curd & Salt Fish Claypot	140
	Chicken & Mushrooms in Plum Sauce	72
	Chrysanthemum Crystal Chicken	138
	Crisp Skin Chicken	71
	Drunken Chicken	65

Hot Diced Chicken in Ground Cashew Nuts	137
Hoi Sin Chicken	68
Lemon Chicken	73
Lychee Mandarin Duck	75
Pine Leaves Tea Smoked Duck	77
Red & Green Chicken Salad with Mustard Dressing	136
Roast Cantonese Chicken	69
Sichuan Spicy Chicken & Peanuts	134
Spicy Chicken Drumsticks or Wings	67
White Cut Chicken with Ginger & Spring Onion Dip	70
Prawn Balls & Snow Peas	60
Prawn Omlette	102
Prawn Stuffed Bean Curd	95
Prawn Stuffed Mushrooms	62

R
Red & Green Chicken Salad with Mustard Dressing	136
Red Simmered Fish	64
Rice:	
Cantonese Fried	29
Hainan Chicken	31
Jook	30
Steamed	28
Roast Cantonese Chicken	69

S
Satay Prawns	55
Sauteed Squid with Capsicums & Onions	50
Seafood:	
Cantonese King Prawns	139
Chicken, Bean Curd & Salt Fish Claypot	140
Crisp Fried Garfish	59
Crispy Prawn Balls	52
Fish Ball Soup	122
Fish Fillets with Spicy Sweet & Sour Sauce Dip	124
Fried Fish Rolls	49
Grape Cluster Fish	58
Imperial Prawns	53
Prawn Balls & Snow Peas	60
Prawn Stuffed Mushrooms	62
Red Simmered Fish	64
Satay Prawns	55
Sauteed Squid with Capsicums & Onions	50
Seafood in Claypot	57
Simplicity Ginger Fish	63
Sliced Fish & Seasonal Vegetables	56
Sliced Fish in Wine Sauce	125
Steamed Black Bean Fish	51
Stir-fried Prawns & Broccoli	54
Stuffed King Prawns	61
Seafood & Spinach Soup	43
Seafood in Claypot	57
Sesame Doughnuts	110
Sesame Prawn Toast	109
Shantung Potatoes	133
Shredded Pork & Leeks with Sichuan Pickles	131
Shrimp Tossed Zucchini	98
Sichuan Spicy Chicken & Peanuts	134
Simplicity Ginger Fish	63
Singapore Noodles	34
Sliced Fish & Seasonal Vegetables	56
Sliced Fish in Wine Sauce	125
Snake Beans in Sichuan Sauce	91
Snow Peas, Straw Mushrooms & Pinenuts	96
Soups:	
Beef & Chinese Turnip	40
Chicken & Asparagus	48

Chicken, Shrimp & Mushroom	38
Chicken Stock	37
Chicken Wine	45
Chinese Cabbage & Bean Curd	40
Combination	44
Fish	42
Fish Ball Soup	122
Fresh Peas & Pork Balls	47
Noodle	41
Oyster Cakes	127
Pork Stock	38
Seafood & Spinach	43
Sour Hot Soup	123
Velvet Chicken & Sweet Corn Soup	46
Winter Melon	43
Won Ton in Chicken	39
Sour Hot Soup	123
Soy Sauce Eggs	101
Spicy Chicken Drumsticks or Wings	67
Spicy Ginger Beef	84
Spring Onion Brushes	67
Spring Onion Cakes	103
Spring Rolls	104
Steamed Black Bean Fish	51
Steamed Pork Dumplings	105
Steamed Rice	28
Steamed Spareribs in Chilli & Black Bean Sauce	81
Stir-fried Bean Sprouts with Celery	98
Stir-fried Prawns & Broccoli	54
Stuffed King Prawns	61
Sweet Bean Pancakes	116
Sweets:	
Almond Cream & Fruits	111
Banana Fritters	112
Coconut Rice Balls	114
Eight Treasure Pudding	113
Sesame Doughnuts	110
Sweet Bean Pancakes	116
Toffee Apples	115
Sweet & Sour Pork	79

T

Tea Leaf Eggs	101
Toffee Apples	115
Tung Po Red Cooked Lamb	130

V Vegetables:

Asparagus & Crab Meat	92
Bacon & Potatoes	97
Bean Curd & Vegetables	99
Bean Curd Salad	128
Buddhist Heavenly Vegetables	93
Cellophane Vermicelli, Ham & Cabbage	97
Gingered Cucumber & Carrots	127
Ma Po Bean Curd	126
Pork or Beef Stirred Cauliflower	94
Prawn Stuffed Bean Curd	95
Shantung Potatoes	133
Shrimp Tossed Zucchini	98
Snake Beans in Sichuan Sauce	91
Snow Peas, Straw Mushrooms & Pinenuts	96
Stir-fried Bean Sprouts with Celery	98
Velvet Chicken & Sweet Corn Soup	46

W

Watercress Soup	49
White Cut Chicken with Ginger & Spring Onion Dip	70
Winter Melon Soup	43
Won Ton in Chicken Soup	39